W9-API-283

SPECTRUM®

Sight Words

Grade 1

Spectrum®
An imprint of Carson-Dellosa Publishing LLC
P.O. Box 35665
Greensboro, NC 27425 USA

© 2015 Carson-Dellosa Publishing LLC. Except as permitted under the United States Copyright Act, no part of this publication may be reproduced, stored, or distributed in any form or by any means (mechanically, electronically, recording, etc.) without the prior written consent of Carson-Dellosa Publishing LLC. Spectrum® is an imprint of Carson-Dellosa Publishing LLC.

Printed in the U.S.A. • All rights reserved.

ISBN 978-1-4838-1189-5

02-227147811

Table of Contents

Notes to Parents and Teachers 4

Sight Word Vocabulary

am, big, box 5
ran, let, got 6
play, ball, hat 8
call, jump, sat 9
red, black, yellow, green 11
white, blue, brown, color 12
say, ask, friend 14
way, may, today 15
girl, look, find 17
dog, run, sit, yes 18
four, five, six, seven, eight 20
nine, ten, money, buy 21
under, upon, next, near 23
high, tree, found 24
until, into, same 26
hard, part, round 27
fat, funny, might 29
saw, only, such, never 30
live, house, home 32
mother, sister, brother 33
each, own, name 35
year, also, fall 36
sleep, morning, night, bed 38
o'clock, early, school 39
open, close, leave 41
off, door, don't 42
read, book, over 44
another, because 45
car, far, ride, around 47
back, away, town, took 48
every, anything, think 50
people, could, too 51
men, woman, along 53
stop, both, walk 54
clean, wash, water 56
carry, hot, warm 57
clothes, coat, cold 59
kind, dress, better 60
please, tell, once 62

Table of Contents

use, made 63
fly, fast, goes 65
try, though, why 66
food, ate, full 68
most, more, always 69
write, letter, dear, love 71
yesterday, soon, fine 73
cut, grow, longer, keep 75
want, than, should 76
these, thing, while 78
which, set 79
first, second, third 81
last, order, stand 82
where, does, those 84
now, seem, shall 85
eyes, ear, hear 87
face, hand, head 88
fire, sure, start 90
hold, show, hope 91
right, left, myself 93
help, small, pair 94
came, gave, pretty 96
present, bring, sing 97
happy, wish, thank 99
didn't, end, best 100

Sight Word Cloze Sentences 102

Sight Word Scrambled Sentences 112

Sight Word Flash Cards 117

Fry Instant Sight Word Lists 145

Answer Key 148

Notes to Parents and Teachers

Whenever a young child reads, 50 to 75% of the words he or she comes across are from the Fry Instant Sight Word List. This is a highly respected, research-based list of the 300 most frequently used words in the English language. Typically, these high-frequency words do not follow regular phonics patterns or spelling rules, making them very difficult for young children to sound out or decode. Consequently, learning to recognize these words immediately "by sight" is a critical first step to successful, confident, fluent reading.

Spectrum Sight Words for First Grade, and its companion, ***Spectrum Sight Words for Kindergarten***, introduce, practice, and review all of the words on this list to help children develop sight word mastery, confidence, and fluency as they encounter these words in both reading and writing. ***Spectrum Sight Words*** are intended for use in school programs or at home with 5-, 6-, and 7-year-olds. The contents are also suitable for older children needing more practice, or for younger children developing early reading skills.

Follow these helpful steps when using this book:

- Follow the exact sequence of the book's exercises, as each sight word is introduced—and then reviewed—in its specific order on the Fry Instant Sight Word List, beginning with the most frequently appearing words.
- Encourage your child to work at his or her own pace, and offer support and praise as he or she completes the exercises.
- Use the sight word flash card pages at the back of the book to create a set of flash cards for practice in reading and writing the sight words.
- Take advantage of the blank flash cards to personalize your child's flash card set.
- Review and evaluate sight word memory by having your child use the sight words in context, using the cloze sentence activities.
- Help your child develop and demonstrate sentence sense by using the scrambled sentence activities to reorganize sight words in correct sentence order.

As teachers and parents, it is our goal to support and foster the learning of all of our children. Activities and materials in ***Spectrum Sight Words for First Grade*** help meet those needs by promoting the appropriate pacing and challenge that allows each child to master reading success.

NAME Willa

Target words: am, big, box

Directions: Write the words below. Say them as you write them.

am	am
big	big
box	box

Directions: Write the missing word in each sentence.

1. I am good at playing with my dog.

2. My dog is big.

3. He is in a box.

Now, write a sentence with these words in it: **big** **box**

I got a big box of toys for my birthday.

NAME _____

Target words: ran, let, got

Directions: Write the words below. Say them as you write them.

ran	ran
let	let
got	got

Directions: Write the missing word in each sentence.

1. I got a dog.

2. He ran in the yard.

3. I let him lick me.

Now, write a sentence with these words in it: **dog - got**

I got up early to feed the dog

NAME _____

Target words: am, big, box, ran, let, got

Directions: Find and circle the words from the box. Words can go → or ↓.

~~am~~
~~big~~
~~box~~
~~ran~~
~~let~~
~~got~~

b	o	x	s	l
i	r	u	n	t
g	a	m	g	o
t	n	r	o	n
e	l	e	t	o

Directions: Draw a line to connect the words that rhyme.

ran	hot
box	fox
got	can

NAME _____

Target words: play, ball, hat

Directions: Write the words below. Say them as you write them.

play	play
ball	ball
hat	hat

Directions: Circle the word that rhymes with the underlined word in each sentence.

1. The boy can <u>play</u>. — day dog pup
2. He has a <u>ball</u>. — bat tall bug
3. He has a <u>hat</u>. — hot bat ball

NAME _____

Target words: call, jump, sat

Directions: Write the words below. Say them as you write them.

call	call
jump	jump
sat	sat

Directions: Write the missing word in each sentence.

1. The frog can jump.
2. He sat by the pond.
3. I will not call to him.
4. paul rhymes with **ball**.

NAME _____

Target words: play, ball, hat, call, jump, sat

Directions: Circle each set of footballs that have rhyming words on them.

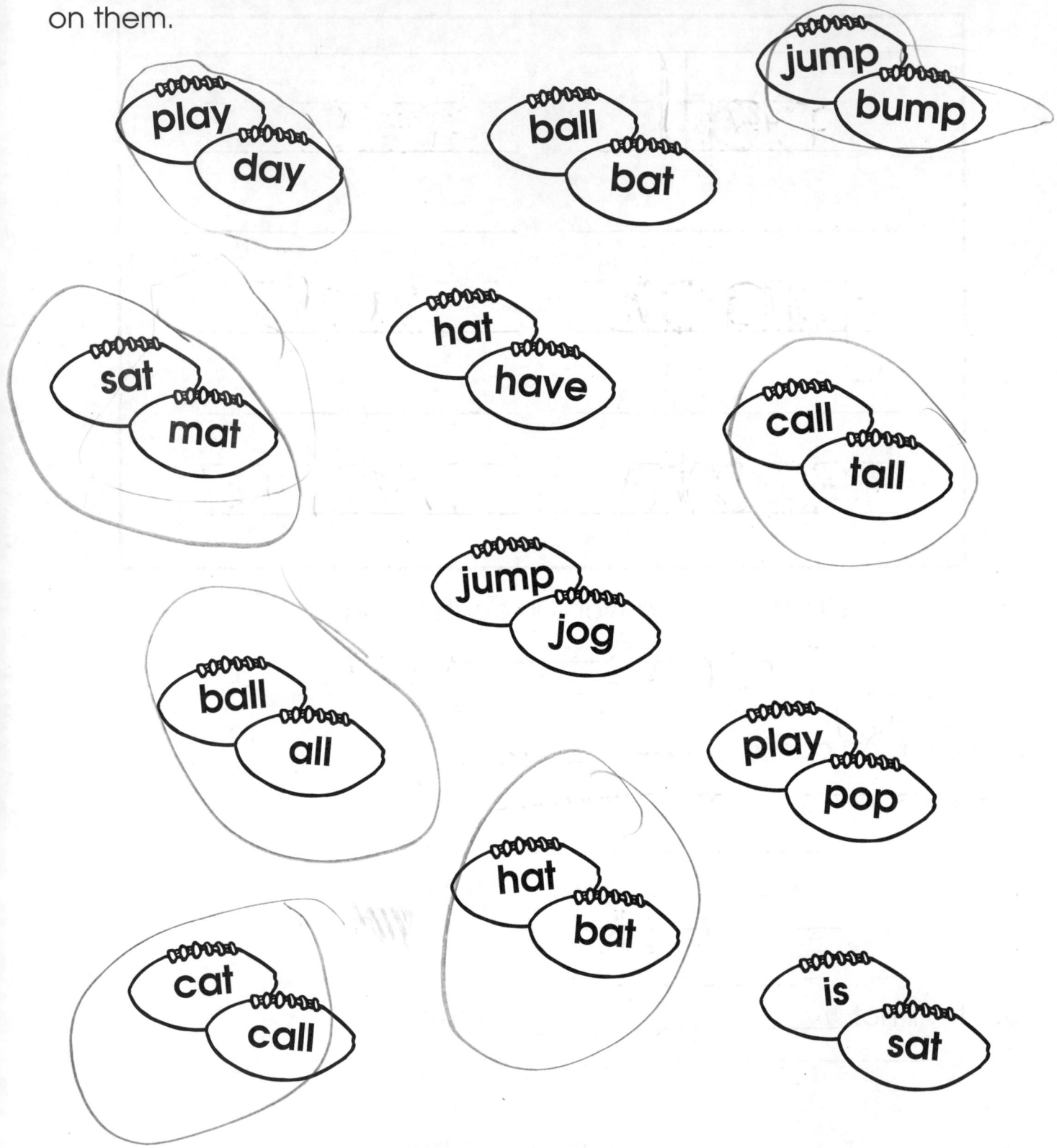

NAME _____

Target words: red, black, yellow, green

Directions: Write the words below. Say them as you write them.

red	red
black	black
yellow	yellow
green	green

Directions: Write the missing word in each sentence.

1. A bear is black.

2. An apple is red.

NAME _____

Target words: white, blue, brown, color

Directions: Write the words below. Say them as you write them.

white	white
blue	blue
brown	brown
color	color

Directions: Write the missing word in each sentence.

white **blue** **brown** **color**

1. I can color the bear brown.

2. The snowman is white.

NAME _____

Target words: **red, black, yellow, green, white, blue, brown, color**

Directions:

1. Color bear number 1 blue.
2. Color bear number 2 green.
3. Color bear number 3 brown.
4. Color bear number 4 yellow.
5. Color bear number 5 white.
6. Color bear number 6 black.
7. Color bear number 7 red.

1

2

3

4

5

6

7

NAME _____

Target words: say, ask, friend

Directions: Write the words below. Say them as you write them.

say	say
ask	ask
friend	friend

Directions: The words **say, ask,** and **friend** are hiding in the lines below. Find and circle them. Now, color the boxes.

a	s	a	y	a	s	a	y	s	a	a	s	a	y	s	y

s	a	k	s	a	s	k	a	s	s	a	s	k	a	s	k

r	e	i	n	d	f	r	i	e	n	d	f	r	e	n	d

NAME _____

Target words: way, may, today

Directions: Write the words below. Say them as you write them.

way way

may may

today today

Directions: Write the missing word in each sentence. Now, circle the words in each sentence that rhyme.

1. This is the way I want to play.
2. today I say this?
3. May is Monday.

Directions: Write 3 more words that rhyme with **way** and **may**.

Pay play

NAME _____

Target words: say, ask, friend, way, may, today

Directions: The letters in the words are mixed up. Unscramble them to write each word correctly. Use the words from the box to help you.

today	way	ask	say	friend

1. ksa — ask
2. yas — say
3. drfeni — friend
4. doayt — today
5. wya — way

Directions: Unscramble the words in this sentence. Now, write the sentence.

I play with my drfeni.

I play with my friend

NAME _____

Target words: girl, look, find

Directions: Write the words below. Say them as you write them.

girl	girl
look	look
find	find

Directions:

1. Circle the box that says **look**.
2. Color the box that says **find**.
3. Put an **X** on the box that says **girl**.

Directions: Circle the two words in each row that are the same.

love	look	like	look
find	four	five	find
girl	girl	got	goat

NAME _____

Target words: dog, run, sit, yes

Directions: Write the words below. Say them as you write them.

dog	dog
run	run
sit	sit
yes	yes

Directions: Find and circle the dog bones with the words from the box on them.

dog	run	sit	yes

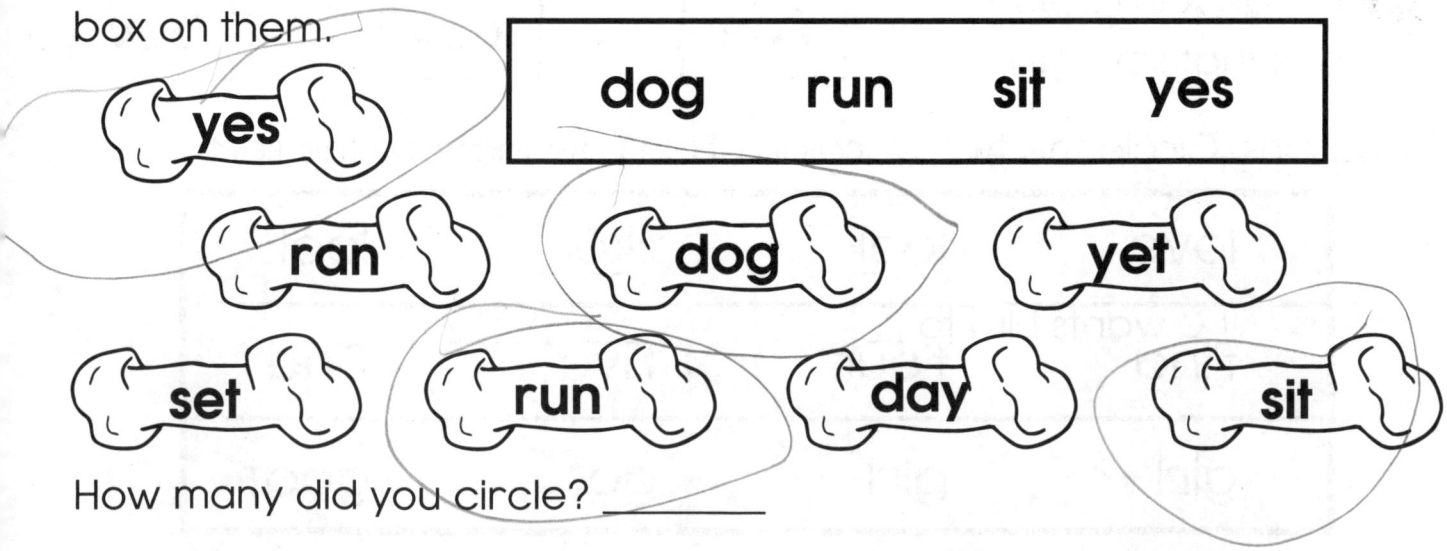

How many did you circle? _____

NAME _____

Target words: girl, look, find, dog, run, sit, yes

Directions: Use the words from the box to write the missing word in each sentence.

girl	look	find	dog	run	sit	yes

1. A _____ had a dog.
2. He liked to _____ fast.
3. One day she lost her _____.
4. She could not _____ him.
5. She had to _____ for him. Did she find him?
6. _____, she did.
7. Now she wants him to _____.

NAME _____

Target words: four, five, six, seven, eight

Directions: Write the words below. Say them as you write them.

four

five

six

seven

eight

Directions: Draw a line to the number that matches the word.

six	4
four	8
five	6
seven	5
eight	7

NAME _____

Target words: nine, ten, money, buy

Directions: Write the words below. Say them as you write them.

nine

ten

money

buy

Directions: Write the missing word in each sentence. Then, write the answers.

1. Can she _____ a pencil?

2. How much _____ does she have?

NAME _____

Target words: **four, five, six, seven, eight, nine, ten, money, buy**

Directions: Draw a line from each box to the word that tells how many coins there are.

nine

five

seven

four

eight

ten

six

NAME _____

Target words: under, upon, next, near

Directions: Write the words below. Say them as you write them.

under

upon

next

near

Directions: Write the missing word in each sentence.

1. The rock is _____ a tree.

2. The frog sits _____ a lily pad.

3. The mouse is _____ to the elephant.

NAME _____

Target words: high, tree, found

Directions: Write the words below. Say them as you write them.

high

tree

found

Directions: Unscramble the letters to make the words from the box. Now, write the correct word next to each apple.

NAME _____

Target words: under, upon, next, near, high, tree, found

Directions: Read each sentence. Now, write it on the line.

The boy ran next to his dog.

_____

_____

They sat upon a bench.

_____

_____

A rock is under the tree.

_____

_____

He threw it high up.

_____

_____

He found it near the tree.

_____

_____

NAME _____

Target words: until, into, same

Directions: Write the words below. Say them as you write them.

until

into

same

Directions: Color the apples that have the same words on them.

NAME _____

Target words: hard, part, round

Directions: Write the words below. Say them as you write them.

hard

part

round

Directions: Draw a line to connect the bouncing balls to get to the basket. Use the words from the box.

round	hard
part	

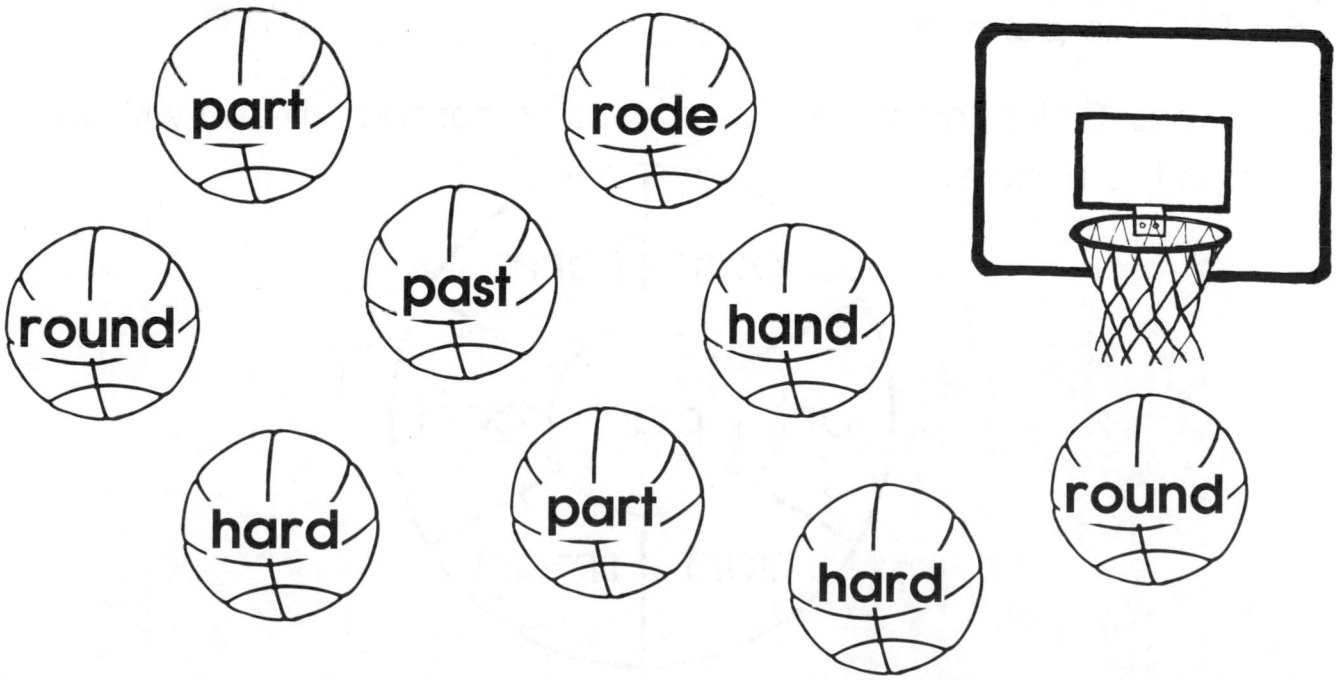

NAME _____

Target words: until, into, same, hard, part, round

Directions: Write the missing word in each sentence.

until	into	same	hard	round

_____

_ _ _ _ _ _ _

1. An apple is _____.

_____

_ _ _ _ _ _ _

2. It is _____.

_____

_ _ _ _ _ _ _

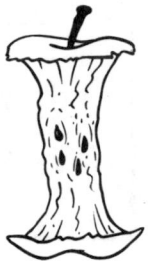

3. You can bite _____ it.

_____

_ _ _ _ _ _ _

4. Eat it all _____ it is gone.

_____

_ _ _ _ _ _ _

5. The two parts are the _____.

Directions: Color the spaces that have words that rhyme with the word in the middle.

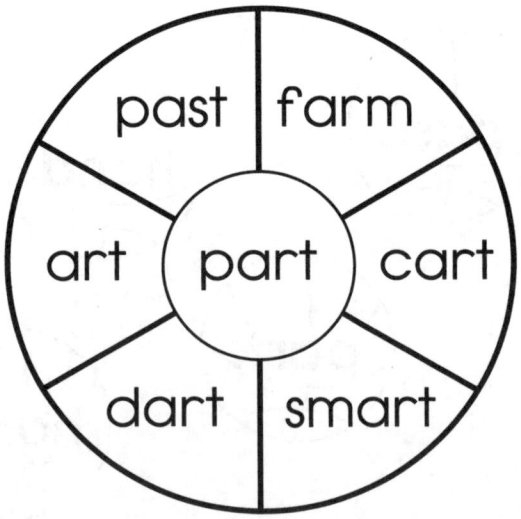

NAME _____

Target words: fat, funny, might

Directions: Write the words below. Say them as you write them.

fat

funny

might

Directions: Draw a line to connect the words that rhyme.

fat	night
funny	bunny
might	cat

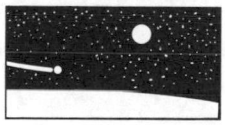

Now, draw a fat, funny mouse.

NAME _____

Target words: saw, only, such, never

Directions: Write the words below. Say them as you write them.

saw

only

such

never

Directions: The words **saw**, **only**, **such**, and **never** are hiding in the boxes below. Find them and color the boxes that have these words in them.

one	only	on	only
saw	was	sun	saw
much	such	such	more
never	ever	never	even

NAME _____

Target words: fat, funny, might, saw, only, such, never

Directions: Find and circle the words from the box. Words can go → or ↓.

fat
funny
might
saw
only
such
never

f	a	t	n	m	n
u	t	i	g	i	e
n	h	v	e	g	v
n	s	u	c	h	e
y	a	n	g	t	r
l	w	o	n	l	y

Directions: Color the spaces that have words that rhyme with the word in the middle of the circle.

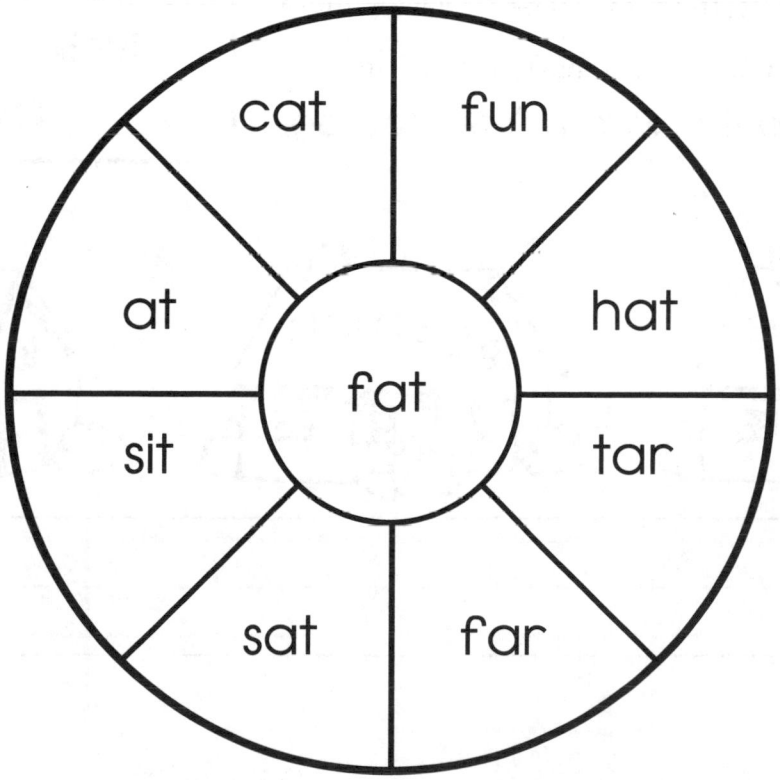

NAME _____

Target words: live, house, home

Directions: Write the words below. Say them as you write them.

live

house

home

Directions: The letters on the houses are mixed up. Unscramble them to write each word. Use the words from the box to help you.

live	house	home

NAME _____

Target words: mother, sister, brother

Directions: Write the words below. Say them as you write them.

mother

sister

brother

Directions: Select the word from the box that answers these riddles.

mother	sister	brother

I am a girl. _____

I am a boy. _____

I am a woman. _____

Now, draw a picture of yourself.

NAME _____

Target words: live, house, home, mother, sister

Directions: Find and circle the words from the box. Words can go ➔ or ↓.

Directions: Draw a picture of where you live.

NAME _____

Target words: each, own, name

Directions: Write the words below. Say them as you write them.

each

own

name

Directions: Read the sentences below and follow the directions.

1. Write your own name on each tag.
2. Color each present blue.
3. What do you think is in the boxes?

NAME _____

Target words: year, also, fall

Directions: Write the words below. Say them as you write them.

year

also

fall

Directions: Read these sentences and draw a picture of them.

Every year the leaves fall.

I like to rake the leaves.

And I also like to jump in them.

NAME _____

Target words: each, own, name, year, also, fall

each	own	name	year	also	fall

Directions: Find the leaves that have the words from the box on them. Color them these colors:

each = red **own** = green **name** = yellow
year = orange **also** = brown

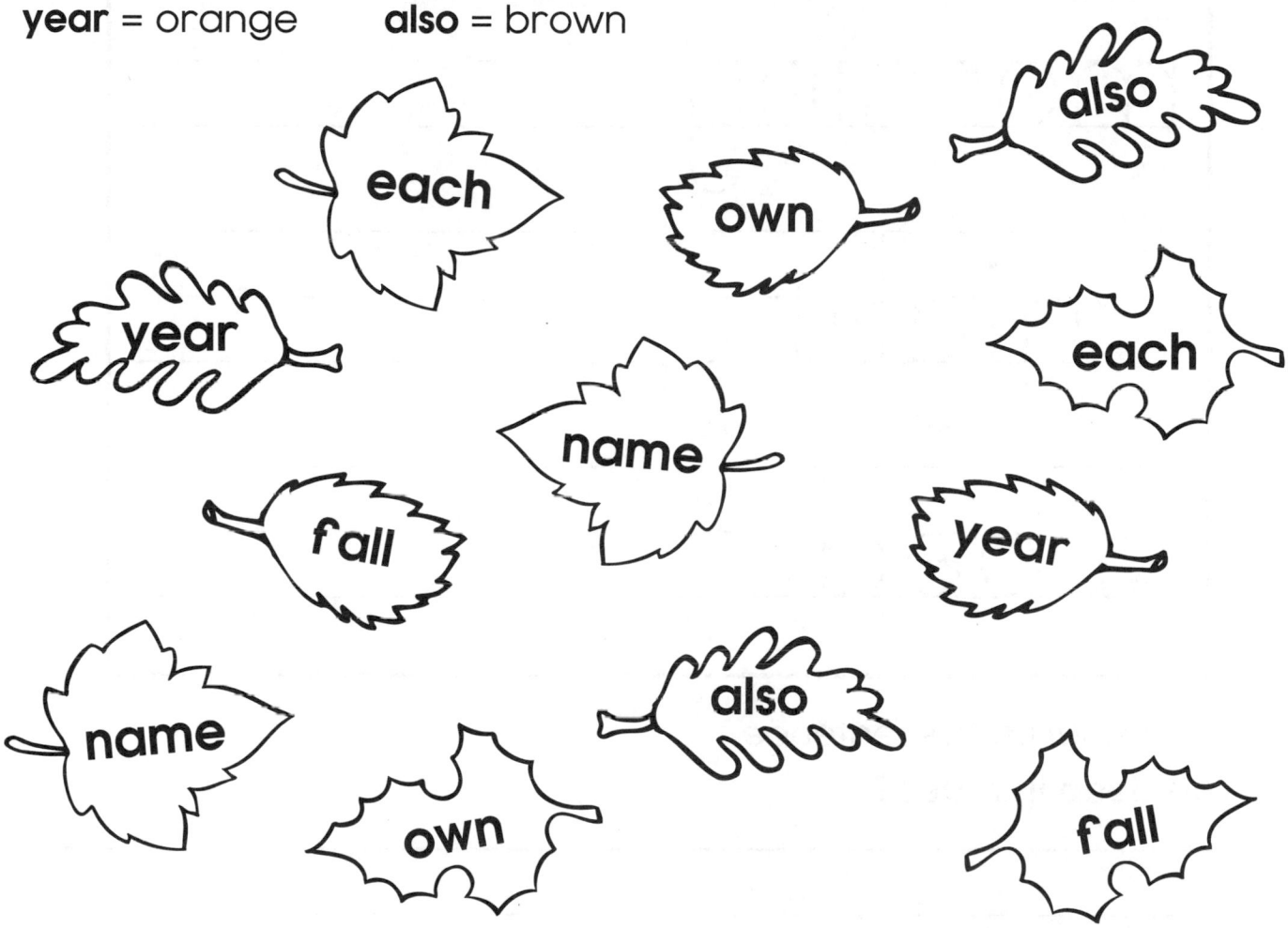

FALL

NAME _____

Target words: sleep, morning, night, bed

Directions: Write the words below. Say them as you write them.

sleep

morning

night

bed

Directions: Write this sentence.

Do you sleep in a bed?

NAME _____

Target words: o'clock, early, school

Directions: Write the words below. Say them as you write them.

o'clock

early

school

Directions: Read the sentences and follow the directions.

1. Write **one** under the star with the word **o'clock** on it.
2. Write **two** under the star with the word **school** on it.
3. Write **three** under the star with the word **early** on it.

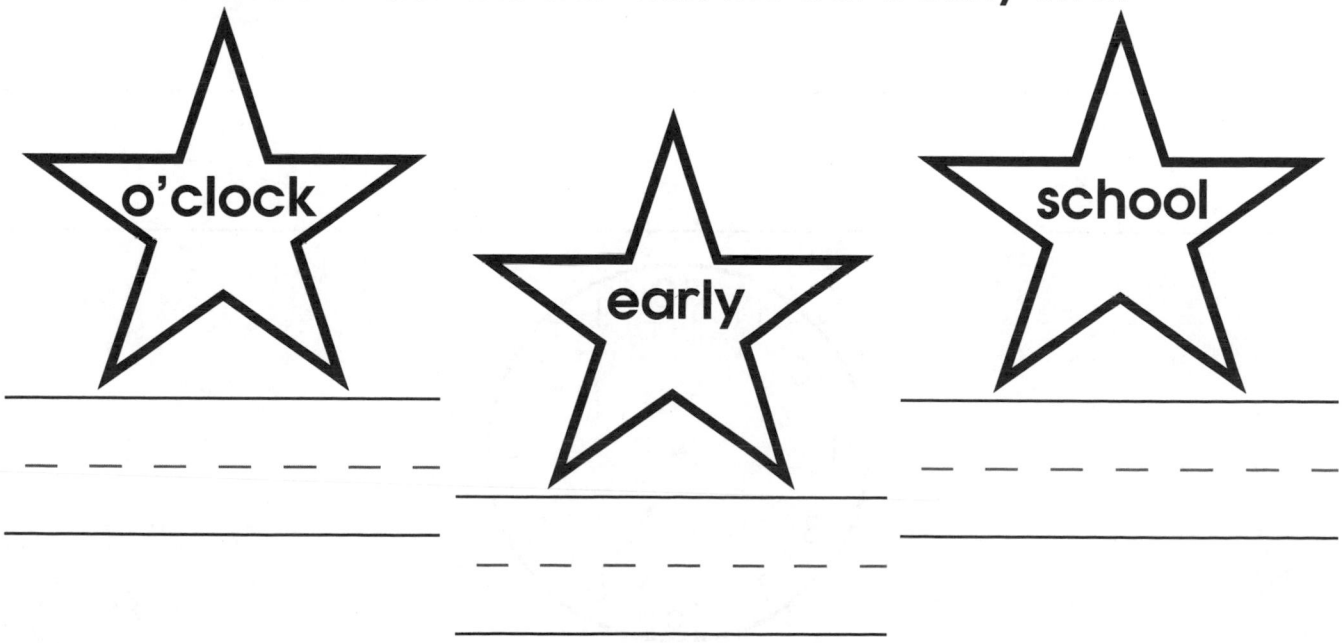

NAME _____

Target words: **sleep, morning, night, bed, o'clock, early, school**

Directions: Read the story. Now, find and circle the words that are in the box.

sleep	**morning**	**night**	**bed**
o'clock	**early**	**school**	

I have to go to bed at eight o'clock at night. I do not like to go to sleep too early. In the morning, I have to get up. When I get up, my dog is there. He wants to go on a walk. So I walk with him before I go to school.

What time do you go to bed? Show it on the clock and write the time on the line.

_____

_____

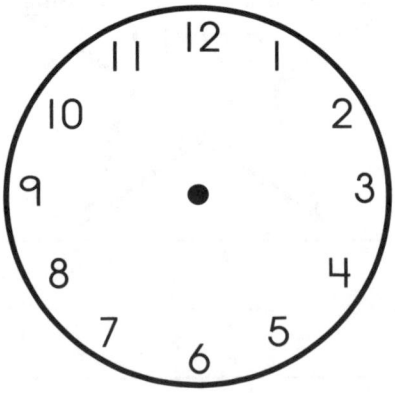

NAME _____

Target words: open, close, leave

Directions: Write the words below. Say them as you write them.

open

close

leave

Directions: Draw a picture of each sentence.

I open the book.

I close the book.

I will leave the book on my bed.

NAME _____

Target words: off, door, don't

Directions: Write the words below. Say them as you write them.

off

door

don't

Directions: Write the missing word in each sentence. Use the words from the box to help you.

off	door	don't

1. I will turn _____ the light.

2. _____ close the door.

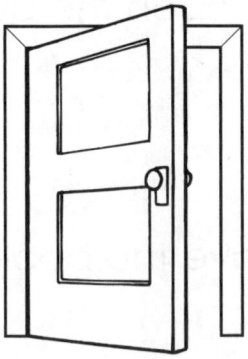

3. The _____ is open.

NAME _____

Target words: open, close, leave, off, door, don't

Directions: Read the story. Now, find and circle the words from the box.

open	close	leave
off	door	don't

One night I had to leave the door open. I do not like the dark, so I said, "Mom, don't close the door." Then I said, "Don't turn the light off." Then I went to sleep.

Directions: Draw a line to connect words that are opposites.

NAME _____

Target words: read, book, over

Directions: Write the words below. Say them as you write them.

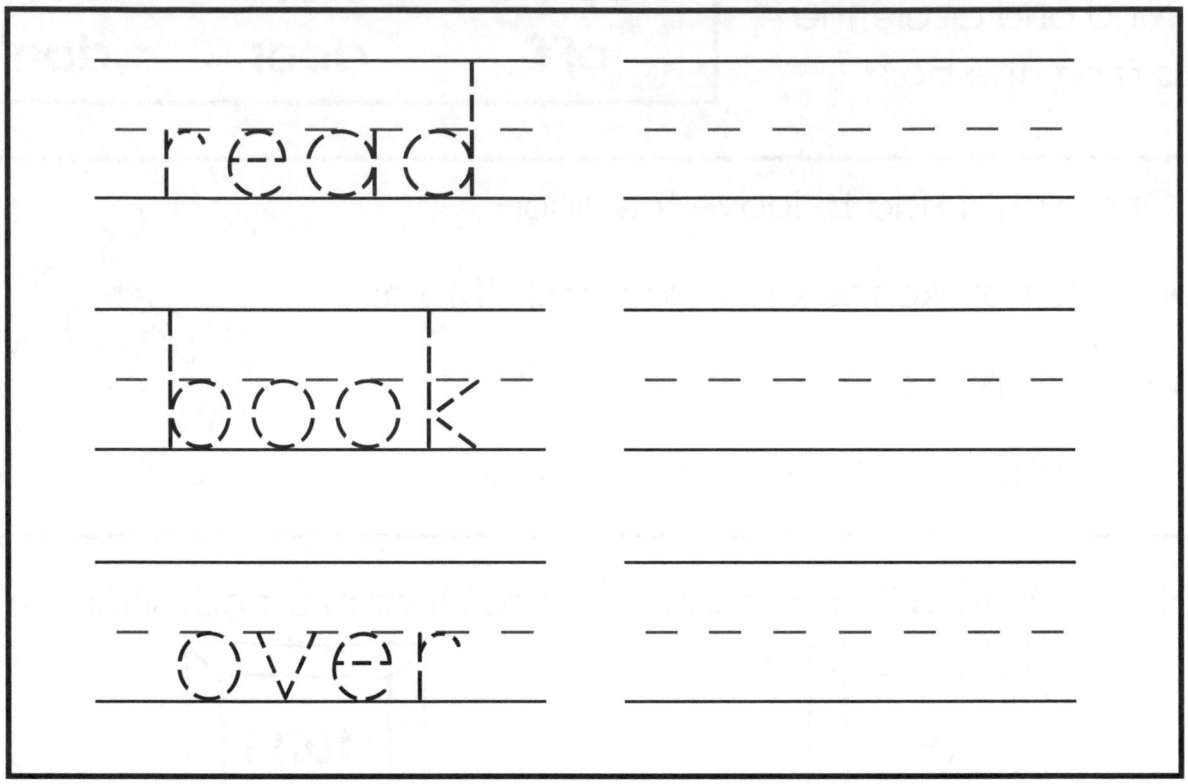

Directions: Several words below are mixed up. Unscramble the letters and write all the words on the lines. Use the words from the box.

book	over	read	and	can	I	a

I _____ nac _____ daer _____ a _____ kobo _____

voer _____ dna _____ voer. _____

NAME _____

Target words: another, because

Directions: Write the words below. Say them as you write them.

another

because

Directions: Draw a picture for each sentence.

I want another dog.

I am hot because the sun is out.

Let's get another pumpkin.

I am cold because I lost my shoes.

NAME _____

Target words: read, book, over, another, because

Directions: Use the words from the box to complete the story.

read	book	over
another	because	

The girl is sitting in a chair. She likes to _____

_____

her _____ here. She will even

_____

read _____ book, too. She has lots of books

_____

_____ she likes to read. She will read her

_____

books _____ again.

Directions: Circle the books with the same words on them.

NAME _____

Target words: car, far, ride, around

Directions: Write the words below. Say them as you write them.

car

far

ride

around

Directions: Color the cars that have words that rhyme with **ride**.

NAME _____

Target words: back, away, town, took

Directions: Write the words below. Say them as you write them.

back

away

town

took

Directions: Read each sentence. Circle the word that rhymes with the underlined word.

1. The car went <u>back</u> home. bag sack come
2. Will the bug go <u>away</u>? rug till stay
3. We went all over <u>town</u>. too down ball
4. It took a <u>long</u> time to get home. lot look song

NAME _____

Target words: **car, far, ride, around, back, away, town, took**

Directions: Find and circle the words from the box. Words can go → or ↓.

k	r	a	t	o	o	k
r	d	k	o	o	t	s
f	a	r	d	w	o	r
a	w	o	f	e	w	i
c	a	r	o	u	n	d
y	y	l	r	t	b	e

Directions: The words **town** and **ride** are hiding in the boxes below. Find and circle them.

w	n	t	o	w	n	t	o	n	w	o	t	o	w	n

e	d	r	i	d	e	r	i	d	r	i	d	e	e	d	e

NAME _____

Target words: every, anything, think

Directions: Write the words below. Say them as you write them.

every

anything

think

Directions: Color the spaces that have the same word as the one in the middle of the circle.

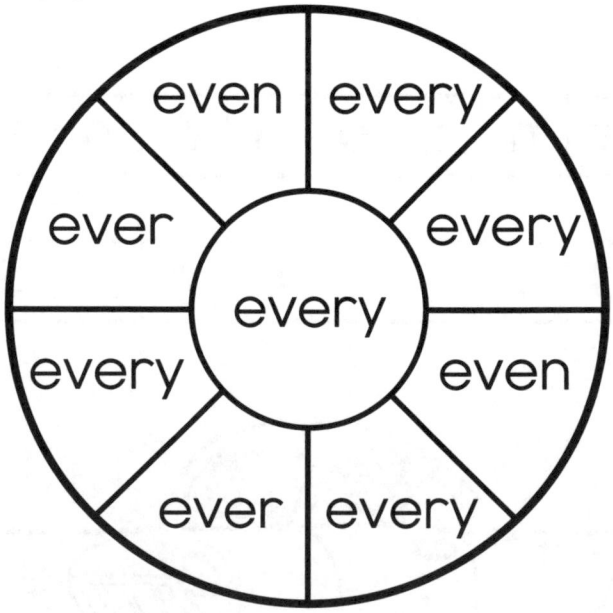

How many spaces did you color? _____

NAME _____

Target words: people, could, too

Directions: Write the words below. Say them as you write them.

people

could

too

Directions: Unscramble the letters to make the words from the box. Now, write them on the line under each book.

could	people	too

oto _____

eopple _____

dcluo _____

Now, write this sentence.

People could read too.

_____

_____

NAME _____

Target words: every, anything, think, people, could, too

Directions: Read the story. Now, find and circle the words from the box.

every	anything	think	people	could	too

I love to read every book I can.

I tell my friends that they could, too.

They could read as many books as I do.

I think lots of people could read anything

they want. Let's read!

Now, write a sentence telling what you think people would like to read about.

_____

_____

_____

_____

_____

_____

_____

_____

NAME _____

Target words: men, woman, along

Directions: Write the words below. Say them as you write them.

men

woman

along

Directions: Color the spaces that have the same word as the one in the middle of the circle.

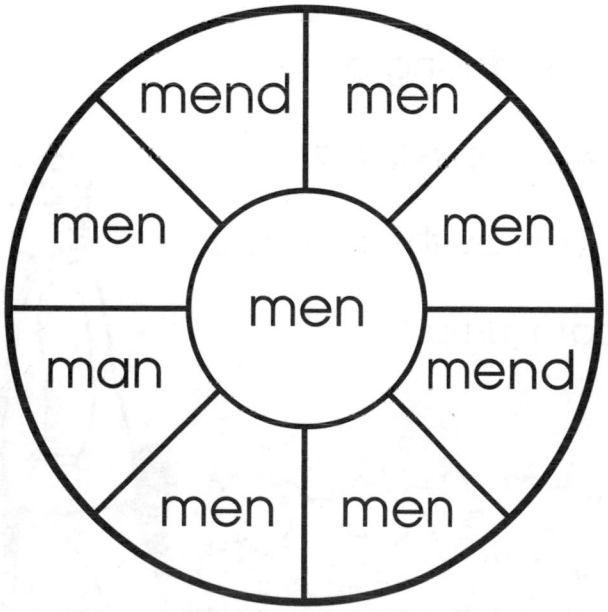

How many spaces did you color? _____

NAME _____

Target words: stop, both, walk

Directions: Write the words below. Say them as you write them.

stop

both

walk

Directions: Look at the picture. Which sentence tells about the picture? Put an **X** by that sentence.

1. _____ Both men are driving a car.
2. _____ Both men will stop eating.
3. _____ Both men walk by the stop sign.
4. _____ The men both jump.

NAME _____

Target words: men, woman, along, stop, both, walk

Directions: To get to the street, draw a line to connect the stop signs that contain the words from the box. The first one is done for you.

men	woman	along	stop	both	walk

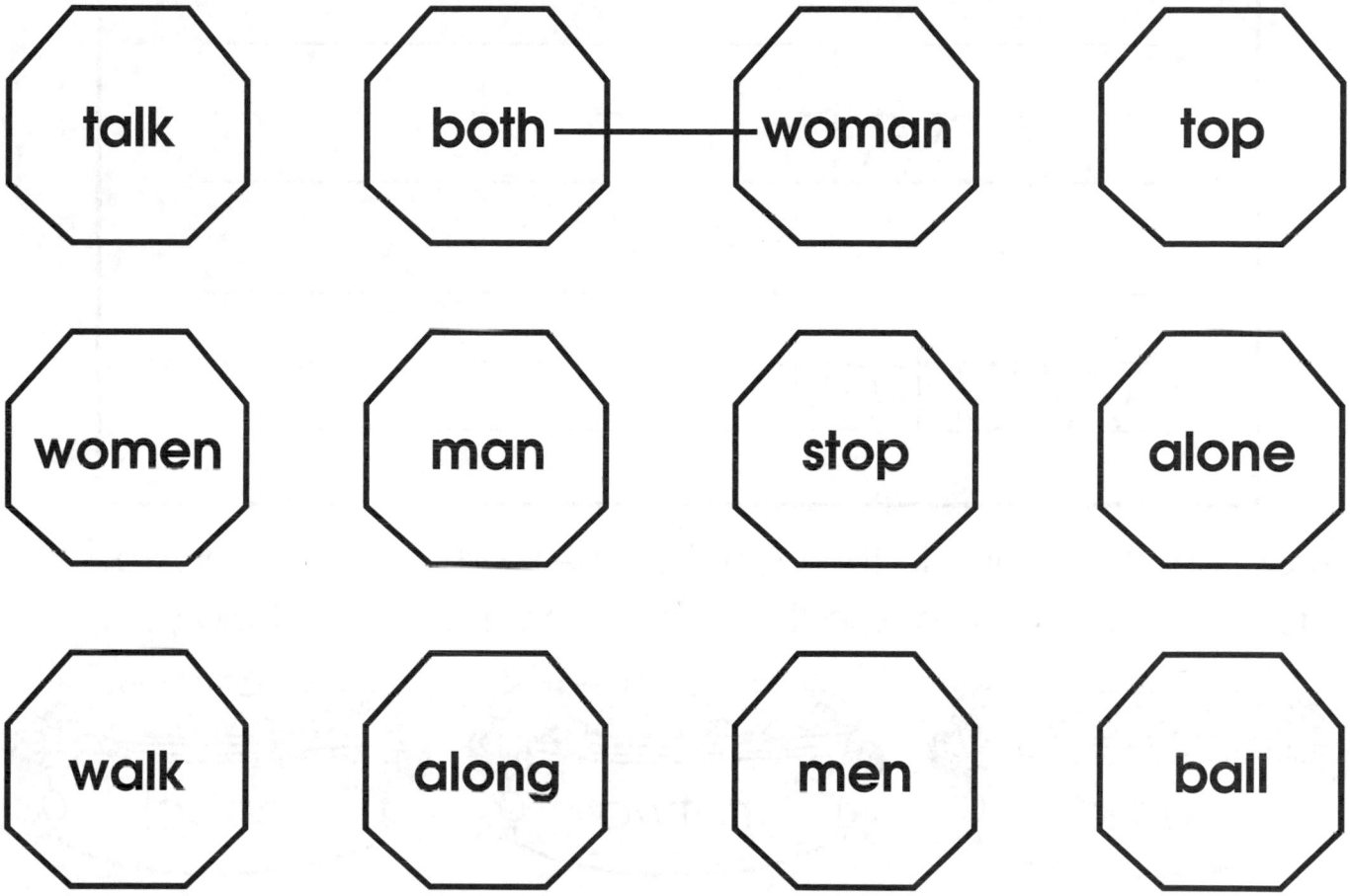

NAME _____

Target words: clean, wash, water

Directions: Write the words below. Say them as you write them.

clean

wash

water

Directions: Unscramble the words on the wash tubs. Now, write each word on the line. Use the words from the box to help you.

Now, write this sentence.

Wash with clean water.

NAME _____

Target words: carry, hot, warm

Directions: Write the words below. Say them as you write them.

carry

hot

warm

Directions: Draw a line from each bucket to its matching word.

carry

hot

water

NAME _____

Target words: clean, wash, water, hot, warm

Directions: Unscramble the words from the box. Write each word on the line under its bubble. Now, write the words on the wash tubs in alphabetical order.

clean	wash	water	hot	warm

naelc

_____

_ _ _ _ _ _ _

_____

hwas

_____

_ _ _ _ _ _ _

_____

rweat

_____

_ _ _ _ _ _ _

_____

toh

_____

_ _ _ _ _ _ _

_____

awrm

_____

_ _ _ _ _ _ _

_____

NAME _____

Target words: clothes, coat, cold

Directions: Write the words below. Say them as you write them.

clothes

coat

cold

Directions: Color the spaces that have words that rhyme with the same word in the middle of the circle.

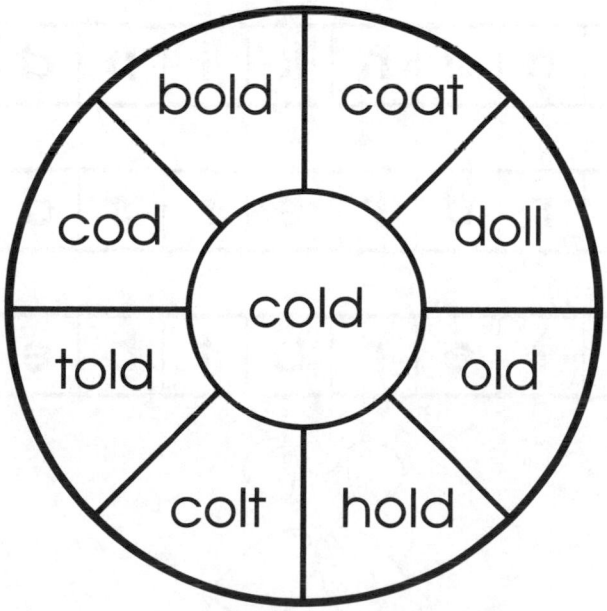

How many spaces did you color? _____

NAME _____

Target words: kind, dress, better

Directions: Write the words below. Say them as you write them.

kind _____

dress _____

better _____

Directions: The words **kind**, **dress**, and **better** are hidden in the lines below. Find and circle them. Now, color the boxes.

k	n	d	k	i	n	d	n	k	i	n	d	n	i	k	n

r	s	e	d	s	r	d	r	e	s	s	d	r	e	s	s

b	e	b	e	t	t	e	r	b	t	b	e	t	t	e	r

NAME _____

Target words: clothes, coat, cold, kind, dress, better

Directions: Find and circle the words from the box. Words can go → or ↓.

clothes
coat
cold
kind
dress
better

r	c	k	i	n	d
b	l	r	c	o	r
e	o	h	o	o	e
t	t	a	a	c	s
t	h	m	t	h	s
e	e	p	e	s	r
r	s	c	o	l	d

Directions: Draw a line to connect each word to its picture.

1. kind
2. coat
3. clothes
4. dress
5. cold
6. better

NAME _____

Target words: please, tell, once

Directions: Write the words below. Say them as you write them.

please

tell

once

Directions: Write the missing word in each sentence. Use the words from the box to help you.

once	tell	please

1. Will you _____ close the door?

2. I can _____ time.

3. _____, I fell in a lake.

NAME _____

Target words: use, made

Directions: Write the words below. Say them as you write them.

use

made

Directions: Write the missing word in each sentence. Use the words from the box to help you.

use	made

1. He _____ a home run hit.

2. I will _____ the bat to hit the ball.

Directions: Color the spaces that have the same word as the one in the middle of the circle.

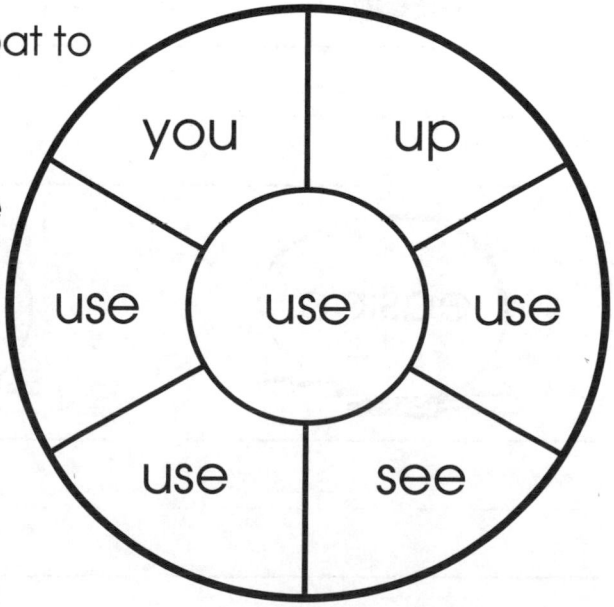

NAME _____

Target words: please, tell, once, use, made

Directions: Read the story. Now, find and circle the words from the box.

once	tell	use	please	made

Once, I wanted to hear a story. I said, "Dad, please tell me one."

Dad said, "Once upon a time, there was a baby duck. It liked to play in the water. Once a day it made a mess. The mother duck said, "That is the last time I let you use the pond to swim in!"

Directions: Unscramble the words on the eggs.

_____

_ _ _ _ _ _ _

_____

_____

_ _ _ _ _ _ _

_____

_____

_ _ _ _ _ _ _

_____

_____

_ _ _ _ _ _ _

_____

_____

_ _ _ _ _ _ _

_____

NAME _____

Target words: fly, fast, goes

Directions: Write the words below. Say them as you write them.

fly

fast

goes

Directions: Color the spaces that have the same word as the one in the middle of the circle.

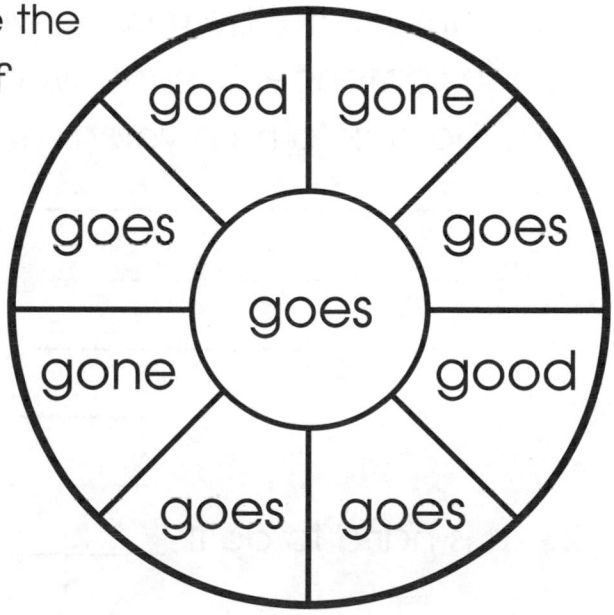

Now, write this sentence.

A plane can fly fast.

NAME _____

Target words: try, though, why

Directions: Write the words below. Say them as you write them.

try

though

why

Directions: Write the missing word in each sentence. Use the words from the box to help you.

try	though	why

1. I _____ to tie my shoes.

2. It is hard to do it _____.

3. I don't know _____ it is hard to do.

NAME _____

Target words: fly, fast, goes, try, though, why

Directions: Find and circle the words from the box. Words can go → or ↓.

s	t	h	o	r	t	w
g	o	e	s	o	e	h
r	y	w	h	t	r	y
a	t	h	o	u	g	h
f	a	s	t	f	a	w
a	o	f	s	l	t	y
w	h	t	r	y	w	h

Directions: Draw a line to connect the planes that have words that rhyme.

NAME _____

Target words: food, ate, full

Directions: Write the words below. Say them as you write them.

food

ate

full

Directions: Write the missing word in each sentence.

food **ate** **full**

1. I like to eat _____.

2. If I eat too much, I get _____.

3. Last night, I _____ too much.

NAME _____

Target words: most, more, always

Directions: Write the words below. Say them as you write them.

most

more

always

Directions: Write the missing letters from the words below. Use the words from the box to help you.

most	more	always

1. mo ____ t
2. a ____ way ____
3. mo ____ e

Now, write a sentence using one of the words from the box.

NAME _____

Target words: food, ate, full, most, more, always

Directions: Find and circle the words from the box. Words can go → or ↓.

a	m	o	r	e	d
l	y	f	e	f	a
w	a	t	e	o	m
a	w	t	m	o	o
y	l	l	u	d	s
s	f	u	l	l	t

Directions: Read the story. Now, find and circle the words from the box.

This food is good. I always eat too much. My dad eats the most. One night he ate it all! Now he is always full. He can not eat any more.

NAME _____

Target words: write, letter, dear, love

Directions: Write the words below. Say them as you write them.

write

letter

dear

love

Directions: Answer the questions below using the words from the box.

letter	dear

1. What do you send in the mail? _____

2. What word do you use to begin a letter? _____

NAME _____

Target words: write

Directions: Color the spaces that have the same word as the one in the middle of the circle.

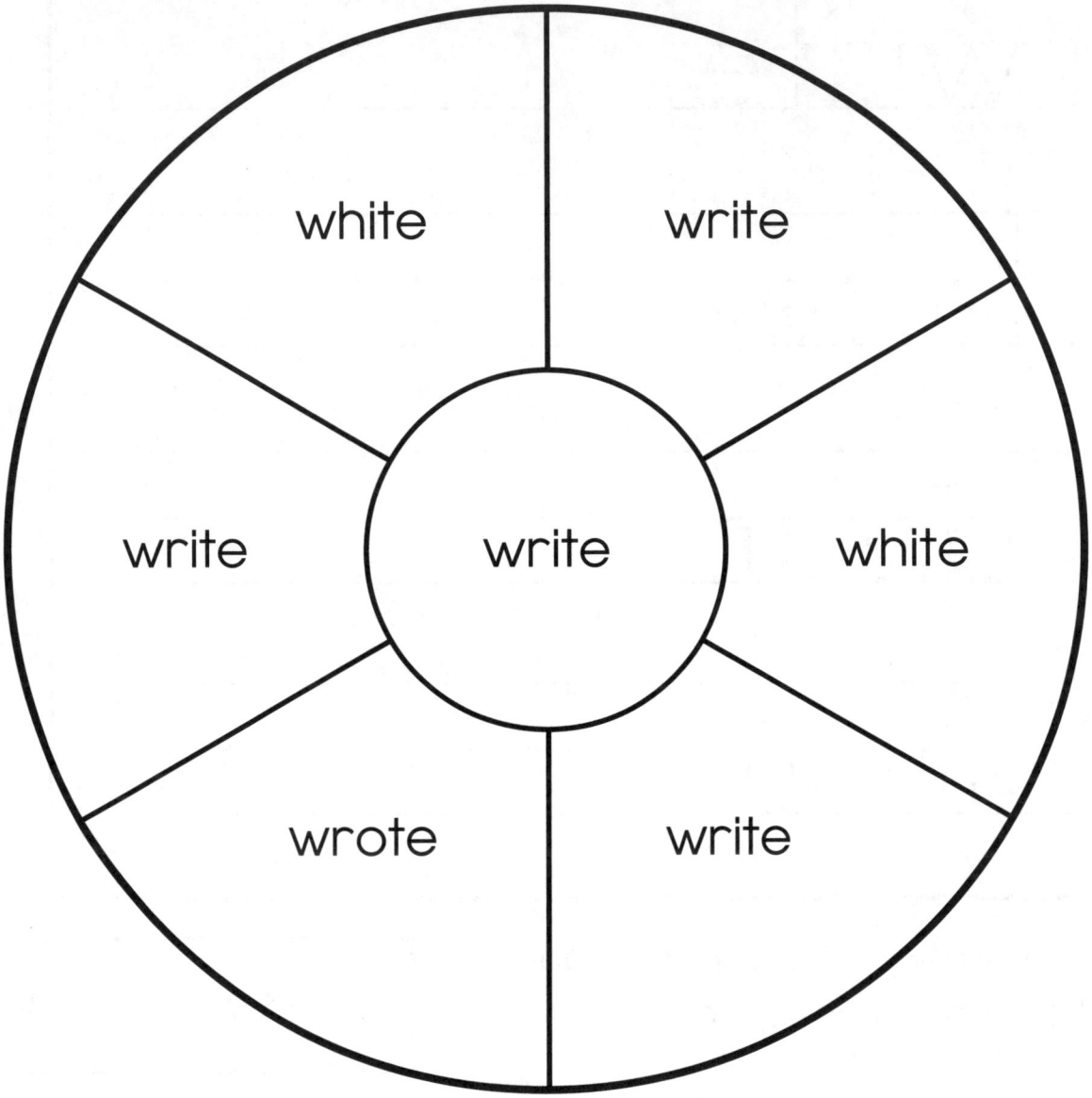

How many did you find? _____

NAME _____

Target words: yesterday, soon, fine

Directions: Write the words below. Say them as you write them.

yesterday

soon

fine

Directions: Circle the word that is the opposite of the underlined word.

1. I went home <u>yesterday</u>.	house	today	no
2. The bus will be here <u>soon</u>.	later	sun	hot
3. We are <u>fine</u>.	sing	song	sick

Now, write this sentence.

I was fine yesterday.

_____

_____

_____

NAME _____

Target words: **write, letter, dear, love, yesterday, soon, fine**

Directions: Find and circle the words from the box that are in the letter.

write	**letter**	**dear**	**love**	**yesterday**	**soon**	**fine**

Dear Grandmother,

I want to write you a letter today because I miss you. I hope you are fine. Yesterday we went to the zoo. See you soon.

Love, Sam

Now, write a note to someone. Use the words **dear**, **love**, **soon**, and **fine**.

NAME _____

Target words: cut, grow, longer, keep

Directions: Write the words below. Say them as you write them.

cut

grow

longer

keep

Directions: Find and circle the words from the box.

cut	grow	longer	keep

gone grow kite

kite cat longer

cat keep

cut gone

NAME _____

Target words: want, than, should

Directions: Write the words below. Say them as you write them.

want

than

should

Directions: Color the spaces that have the same word as the one in the middle of the circle.

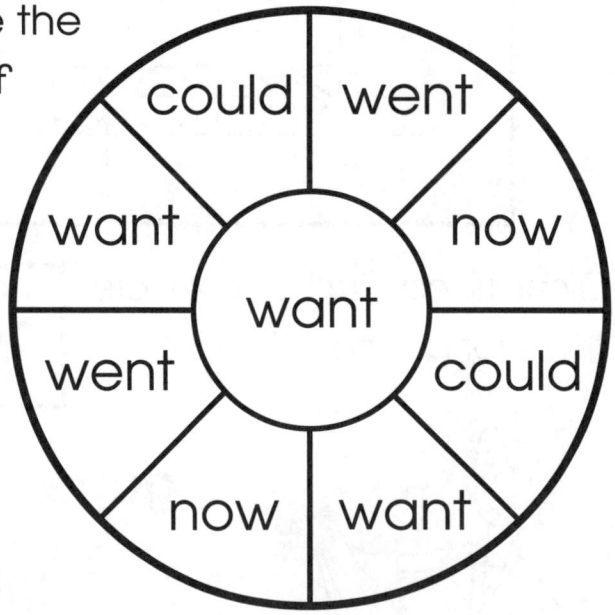

Now, write a sentence using the word **than** or **should**.

_____

_____

_____

NAME _____

Target words: cut, grow, longer, keep, want, than, should

Directions: Read the story. Find and circle the words from the box.

longer	**keep**	**want**	**grow**
should	**cut**	**want**	

I want to cut the grass. I should cut it today because it is going to rain. It is hard to keep it looking good. I want it to grow, but the bugs keep eating it. Maybe it will grow longer next year.

Directions: Write the letters that are missing in the words below. Use the words from the box to help you.

c _____ t

g _____ ow

t _____ a _____

_____ ee _____

sh _____ _____ l _____

lo _____ _____ e _____

w _____ nt

NAME _____

Target words: these, thing, while

Directions: Write the words below. Say them as you write them.

these

thing

while

Directions: The words **these** and **thing** are hidden in the lines below. Find and circle them.

t	h	e	s	t	h	e	s	e	t	h	e	s	t	h	e

t	h	i	n	t	h	n	g	t	h	i	n	g	t	h	n

How many did you circle of each?

these _____ **thing** _____

NAME _____

Target words: which, set

Directions: Write the words below. Say them as you write them.

which

set

Directions: Color the spaces that have the same word as the one in the middle of the circle.

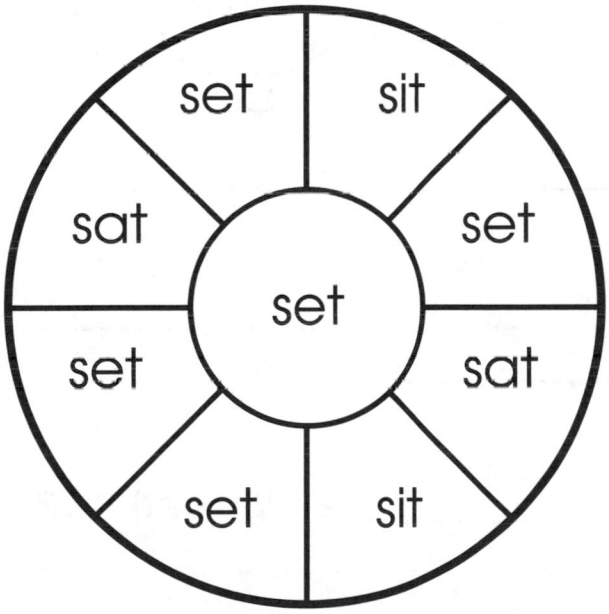

How many spaces did you color? _____

NAME _____

Target words: these, thing, while, which, set

Directions: Put the correct words on the footprints to complete the sentences below.

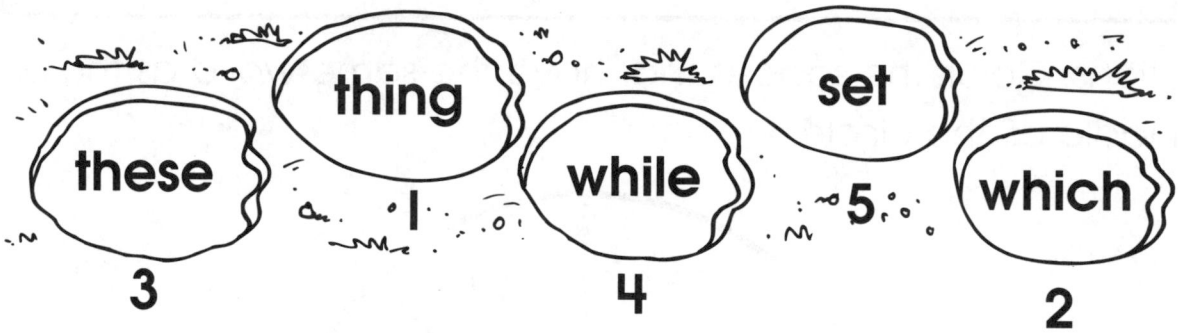

_____ _____

_ _ _ _ _ _ _ _ _ _ _ _ _ _

This _____ is big. _____ animal is

_____

_ _ _ _ _ _ _ _ _ _ _ _ _ _

here? _____ are big feet! I will hide

_____

_ _ _ _ _ _ _ _ _ _ _ _ _ _

_____ it goes by. I do not want it to

_____

_ _ _ _ _ _ _ _ _ _ _ _ _ _

knock over my _____ of blocks.

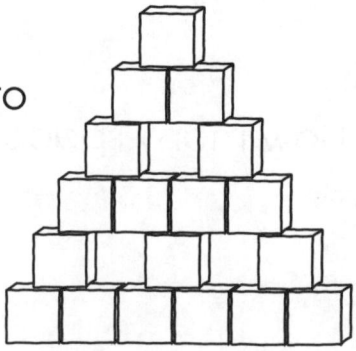

NAME _____

Target words: first, second, third

Directions: Write the words below. Say them as you write them.

first

second

third

Directions: Write the word from the box that tells which football it is.

first	second	third

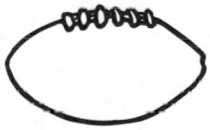

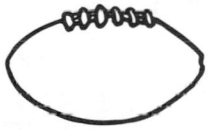

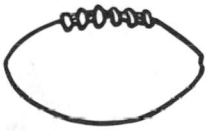

Directions: Answer the question below.

What grade are you in? _____

NAME _____

Target words: last, order, stand

Directions: Write the words below. Say them as you write them.

last

order

stand

Directions: Answer the questions using the words from the box.

order	last	stand

1. Circle the dog that is next to last.
2. Color the dog that is on the stand.
3. The dogs are in order. Draw an arrow to show the tallest and the shortest dogs.

NAME _____

Target words: first, second, third, last, order, stand

Directions: Read the sentences to answer the questions about the picture.

_____

_ _ _ _ _ _ _

1. Who is in the last row? _____

_____

_ _ _ _ _ _ _

2. Who is in the second row? _____

_____

_ _ _ _ _ _ _

3. Who is in the third row? _____

_____

_ _ _ _ _ _ _

4. Who is in the first row? _____

5. Draw where you will stand in the picture.

NAME _____

Target words: where, does, those

Directions: Write the words below. Say them as you write them.

where

does

those

Directions: Write the word from the box that is missing in each sentence below.

where	does	those

1. _____ he have his shoes?

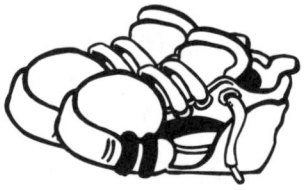

2. Are _____ his socks?

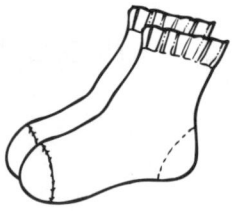

3. _____ is his coat?

NAME _____

Target words: now, seem, shall

Directions: Write the words below. Say them as you write them.

now

seem

shall

Directions: The words **now**, **seem**, and **shall** are hiding in the lines below. Find and circle them. Now, color the boxes.

n	w	o	n	o	w	o	w	n	o	w	n	o	n	o	w

e	m	e	e	m	s	e	e	m	e	e	s	e	e	m	e

s	h	l	l	s	h	a	l	l	s	h	a	l	s	h	a

Directions: What time is it now?

NAME _____

Target words: where, does, those, now, seem, shall

Directions: Write the sentences below.

1. Where are the birds?

2. Does it seem late?

3. No, it doesn't seem late.

4. What time is it now?

5. Who has those shoes?

6. Shall I open the door?

NAME _____

Target words: eyes, ear, hear

Directions: Write the words below. Say them as you write them.

eyes

ear

hear

Directions: Write the word that is missing in each sentence below.

eyes **ear** **hear**

1. I see with my _____.

2. My _____ can help me _____.

Now, draw a picture of your face. Show where your eyes and ears are. Put a label on them.

NAME _____

Target words: face, hand, head

Directions: Write the words below. Say them as you write them.

face

hand

head

Directions: Fill in the letters that are missing in the words below.

1. h _____ n _____
2. f _____ c _____
3. h _____ _____ d

Now, draw a picture of yourself . Show where your face, hands, and head are. Put labels on your drawing.

NAME _____

Target words: eyes, ear, hear, face, hand, head

Directions: Use the words from the box to fill in the labels on the drawing.

eyes	ear	face
hand	head	

Now, write this sentence.

I can hear a train.

_____

_____

_____

NAME _____

Target words: fire, sure, start

Directions: Write the words below. Say them as you write them.

fire

sure

start

Directions: Color the spaces that have the same word as the one in the middle of the circle.

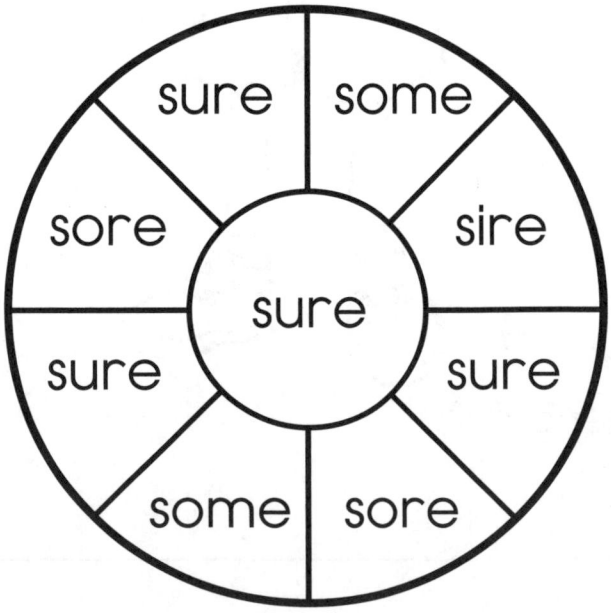

NAME _____

Target words: hold, show, hope, start

Directions: Write the words below. Say them as you write them.

hold _____

show _____

hope _____

Directions: Circle the three words in each row that are the same.

hope	hold	hold	home	hold
shop	ship	show	show	show
home	hope	hope	ham	hope
start	stop	start	store	start

NAME _____

Target words: fire, sure, start, hold, show, hope

Directions: Read the story. Find and circle the words from the box.

start	sure	hold	show	hope	fire

It is cold and time to start a fire. My dad will show us how to start the fire. I hope it gets warm soon. I will hold my hands close to the fire to warm up. My dad says, "Be sure not to get too close."

Now, write this sentence.

I hope he will show us how to hold that.

_____

_____

_____

_____

NAME _____

Target words: right, left, myself

Directions: Write the words below. Say them as you write them.

right

left

myself

Directions: Read the sentences. Now, follow the directions.

1. Circle the dog on the right.
2. Color the dog on the left.
3. Draw an arrow to the cat on the left.
4. Color the cat on the right.

Now, complete this sentence.

_____

I like myself because _____

_____

_____

NAME _____

Target words: help, small, pair

Directions: Write the words below. Say them as you write them.

help

small

pair

Directions: Draw a line to match the pants that have the same words on them.

help	small	pair

Now, write this sentence.

It is a pair of pants.

NAME _____

Target words: right, left, myself, help, small, pair

Directions: Find and circle the words from the box. Words can go → or ↓.

right
left
myself
help
small
pair

m	y	s	e	l	f	f
t	t	l	p	f	r	t
s	m	a	l	l	r	f
g	f	p	e	e	i	e
h	e	l	p	f	g	l
l	s	m	a	t	h	g
p	a	i	r	m	t	h

Directions: Draw a line to connect words that are opposites.

yourself	hurt
right	pair
big	left
one	small
help	myself

Now, draw a picture of one of the opposite pairs.

NAME _____

Target words: came, gave, pretty

Directions: Write the words below. Say them as you write them.

came

gave

pretty

Directions: Write these sentences.

My friend came to my party.

Mother gave me a dress.

I had a pretty cake.

NAME _____

Target words: present, bring, sing

Directions: Write the words below. Say them as you write them.

present

bring

sing

Directions: Color the boxes that have **present**, **bring**, and **sing** in them. Use a different color for each word.

song	present	bang	sing
pretty	bring	song	present
sing	present	bright	sang
present	pretty	sing	bring

How many did you find?

present _____ bring _____ sing _____

NAME _____

Target words: came, gave, pretty, present, bring, sing

Directions: Find and circle the words from the box. Words can go → or ↓.

came
gave
pretty
present
bring
sing

g	a	v	e	r	l	y
o	g	a	e	v	n	p
n	v	s	i	n	g	r
c	a	m	e	o	n	e
a	t	p	r	e	i	t
p	r	e	s	e	n	t
b	r	i	n	g	b	y

Directions: Circle the candles that have the words from the box on them.

How many candles did you circle? _____

NAME _____

Target words: happy, wish, thank

Directions: Write the words below. Say them as you write them.

happy

wish

thank

Directions: Draw a string to tie the balloons together that have the words from the box on them.

happy	wish	thank

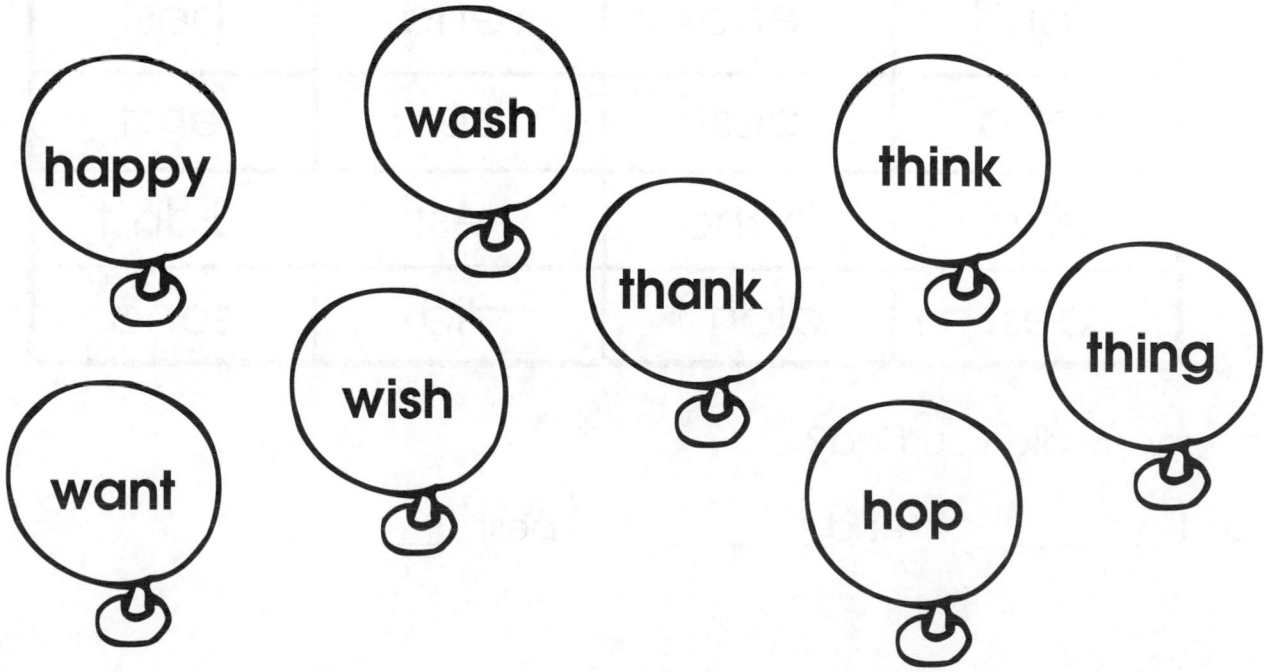

NAME _____

Target words: didn't, end, best

Directions: Write the words below. Say them as you write them.

didn't

end

best

Directions: Color the boxes that have the words **didn't**, **end**, and **best** in them. Use a different color for each word.

don't	end	send	best
send	best	bet	end
end	bend	rest	didn't
best	didn't	did	send

How many did you find?

didn't _____ end _____ best _____

NAME _____

Target words: **came, gave, pretty, present, bring, sing, happy, wish, thank, didn't, end, best**

Directions: Read the story. Now, find and circle the words that are in the box.

came	**gave**	**pretty**	**present**	**bring**	**sing**
happy	**wish**	**thank**	**didn't**	**end**	**best**

It was my birthday. Lots of people came to bring me a present. They also came to sing happy birthday. My mother gave me a pretty dress. My brother gave me a big book. I have to thank them all. I wish the day didn't have to end. It was the best birthday ever!

Now, draw a picture of your favorite birthday present.

NAME _____

Sight Word Cloze Sentences

Cloze sentences provide young learners an opportunity to use words in context and to gain a better understanding of sentence sense. Use the cloze sentences on the following pages for children to practice selecting the correct word from the word boxes to complete each sentence.

To extend the activity, have children create their own sentences with a missing word. The sentences can also be copied on a separate sheet of paper, cut apart, and reconstructed for sentence sense practice.

Directions: Write the missing word in each sentence.

big	box	got	ran	let

_____

_ _ _ _ _ _ _ _ _

1. I _____ a dog.

_____

_ _ _ _ _ _ _ _ _

2. He sleeps in a _____.

_____

_ _ _ _ _ _ _ _ _

3. My dog is _____.

_____

_ _ _ _ _ _ _ _ _

4. He _____ in the yard.

_____

_ _ _ _ _ _ _ _ _

5. I _____ him lick me.

NAME _____

Cloze Sentences

Directions: Write the missing word in each sentence.

girl	look	find	sit	run	yes

_____

_ _ _ _ _ _ _ _ _

1. The _____ had a dog.

_____

_ _ _ _ _ _ _ _ _

2. The dog liked to _____ away fast.

_____

_ _ _ _ _ _ _ _ _

3. The girl had to _____ the dog.

_____

_ _ _ _ _ _ _ _ _

4. She had to _____ for him.

_____

_ _ _ _ _ _ _ _ _

5. Did she find him? _____, she did!

_____

_ _ _ _ _ _ _ _ _

6. Now the girl wants the dog to _____.

NAME _____

Cloze Sentences

Directions: Write the missing word in each sentence.

sleep	bed	morning	school	early	night

_____

_ _ _ _ _ _ _ _ _

1. It is dark at _____.

_____

_ _ _ _ _ _ _ _ _

2. I get in my _____.

_____

_ _ _ _ _ _ _ _ _

3. I have to go to _____ now.

_____

_ _ _ _ _ _ _ _ _

4. In the _____ I get up.

_____

_ _ _ _ _ _ _ _ _

5. I have to get up _____.

_____

_ _ _ _ _ _ _ _ _

6. And I have to go to _____.

NAME _____

Cloze Sentences

Directions: Write the missing word in each sentence.

open	close	leave	door	don't	off

_____

_ _ _ _ _ _ _ _ _

1. I see a _____.

_____

_ _ _ _ _ _ _ _ _

2. It is _____.

_____

_ _ _ _ _ _ _ _ _

3. Don't _____ the door.

_____

_ _ _ _ _ _ _ _ _

4. _____ the light on.

_____

_ _ _ _ _ _ _ _ _

5. Please don't turn _____ the light.

_____

_ _ _ _ _ _ _ _ _

6. I _____ like the dark.

NAME _____

Cloze Sentences

Directions: Write the missing word in each sentence.

car	far	ride	took	around	back

_____

_ _ _ _ _ _ _ _ _

1. We went for a _____.

_____

_ _ _ _ _ _ _ _ _

2. We drove in the _____.

_____

_ _ _ _ _ _ _ _ _

3. The ride _____ a long time.

_____

_ _ _ _ _ _ _ _ _

4. We went _____ away.

_____

_ _ _ _ _ _ _ _ _

5. Then we went _____ the park.

_____

_ _ _ _ _ _ _ _ _

6. At last we came _____ home.

NAME _____

Cloze Sentences

Directions: Write the missing word in each sentence.

done	wash	clean	water	carry	warm

_____

_ _ _ _ _ _ _ _ _

1. I have to _____ the dishes.

_____

_ _ _ _ _ _ _ _ _

2. I will _____ them to the sink.

_____

_ _ _ _ _ _ _ _ _

3. I need to get some _____.

_____

_ _ _ _ _ _ _ _ _

4. The water is not too _____.

_____

_ _ _ _ _ _ _ _ _

5. Now the dishes are _____.

_____

_ _ _ _ _ _ _ _ _

6. Now I am _____!

NAME _____

Cloze Sentences

Directions: Write the missing word in each sentence.

coat	cold	dress	kind	better	clothes

_____

_ _ _ _ _ _ _ _ _

1. It is _____ outside.

_____

_ _ _ _ _ _ _ _ _

2. I _____ not go outside yet.

_____

_ _ _ _ _ _ _ _ _

3. My _____ is not very warm.

_____

_ _ _ _ _ _ _ _ _

4. First, I need to put on some warm _____.

_____

_ _ _ _ _ _ _ _ _

5. My mom gives me a warm _____.

_____

_ _ _ _ _ _ _ _ _

6. She is very _____ to me.

NAME _____

Cloze Sentences

Directions: Write the missing word in each sentence.

more	always	ate	food	full	most

_____

_ _ _ _ _ _ _ _ _

1. The _____ is good here.

_____

_ _ _ _ _ _ _ _ _

2. I _____ eat too much.

_____

_ _ _ _ _ _ _ _ _

3. My dad eats the _____ food.

_____

_ _ _ _ _ _ _ _ _

4. He _____ all the food on his plate!

_____

_ _ _ _ _ _ _ _ _

5. Now he is _____.

_____

_ _ _ _ _ _ _ _ _

6. He can not eat any _____.

NAME _____

Cloze Sentences

Directions: Write the missing word in each sentence.

dear	letter	soon	love	fine	yesterday

_____

_ _ _ _ _ _ _ _ _

1. Bob wrote a _____ to his sister.

_____

_ _ _ _ _ _ _ _ _

2. He wrote, "_____ Pat, how are you?"

_____

_ _ _ _ _ _ _ _ _

3. "I am _____," Bob wrote.

_____

_ _ _ _ _ _ _ _ _

4. "_____ I went to the park."

_____

_ _ _ _ _ _ _ _ _

5. He signed it, "_____, Bob."

_____

_ _ _ _ _ _ _ _ _

6. He will mail it _____.

NAME _____

Cloze Sentences

Directions: Write the missing word in each sentence.

ear	hand	head	eyes	hear	face

_____

_ _ _ _ _ _ _ _ _

1. I can _____ the dog bark.

_____

_ _ _ _ _ _ _ _ _

2. I can hear with my _____.

_____

_ _ _ _ _ _ _ _ _

3. I have two _____.

_____

_ _ _ _ _ _ _ _ _

4. I can see my _____ in the mirror.

_____

_ _ _ _ _ _ _ _ _

5. My hat is on my _____.

_____

_ _ _ _ _ _ _ _ _

6. A _____ has five fingers.

Sight Word Scrambled Sentences

Once children can recognize and understand individual sight words in print, they are ready to use them to build sentences. This is the exciting next step in the reading process and, for many children, the moment when they say, "I'm really reading!"

The following scrambled sentences build upon sight word knowledge and are designed to help children learn—and demonstrate—sentence sense by putting individual words into the correct order so each sentence makes sense. The sight words used in these sentences follow the order in which they have been introduced.

The sentences can be used in a number of ways, depending on each child's developmental level. First, encourage the child to look for helpful sentence-sense clues, such as a capitalized word that would indicate the beginning of the sentence and a word with punctuation that would indicate the end of the sentence. Then, have the child say all the words aloud, starting with the capitalized word and ending with the punctuated word. Ask the child if what he or she said aloud makes sense, and, if necessary, encourage him or her to rearrange the "middle" words around while saying them aloud until they are in the correct order. Then, have the child write the unscrambled sentence on the line provided. You may want to encourage the child to write the sentence's sight words in different-colored crayons or markers, or to use the sight word flash cards to find the matching words used in the sentence.

You may also want to have the child write the unscrambled sentence on a separate sheet of paper and cut it apart into individual words. Then, using the child's hand-written unscrambled sentence in the workbook as a model, have him or her reassemble the cut-apart words into the sentence. This activity works well as a self-checking review. Or have the child distribute the cut-apart words to other children, who can then reassemble them in the correct order. An activity of this type can also be used with sentences that the children dictate or write themselves on a separate sheet of paper. Extending this activity to sentences that children compose themselves increases their level of engagement and provides an opportunity for individualizing their learning.

NAME _____

Scrambled Sentences

say I May this?

_____

likes He fast. run to

_____

him. had to She for look

_____

buy she Can pencil? a

_____

NAME _____

Scrambled Sentences

under tree. rock a A is

_____

_____

will the car. I leave

_____

_____

door. Please the close

_____

_____

get Let's pumpkin. another

_____

_____

_____

_____

NAME _____

Scrambled Sentences

fast. That plane can fly

_____

_____

dad most. the eats My

_____

_____

five hand has fingers. A

_____

_____

letter will write a I you. to

_____

_____

_____

_____

NAME _____

Scrambled Sentences

a He run. hit home

soon write letter. I will a

can I see eyes. with my

goes here. It right

Sight Word Flash Cards

On the following pages are flash cards for all of the sight words used in this book. For ease of use, they are presented in the order of introduction in the book. Laminating the cards would also help make them durable. Punching a hole in each card and keeping them on a ring for each child is also a good way to keep the cards organized and easy to use.

There are many ways to use these cards. Listed below are some games and activities to help children learn to recognize the sight words:

- Sort the cards by sight words with the same beginning letter
- Find sight words that rhyme, and write other words that rhyme with the sight words on a dry erase board or separate sheet of paper.
- Sort the cards to make pairs of sight words that begin with the same letter. Play the "Memory" game using these words—players don't get to keep the pair unless they can read both words. As an extension of this, also have players use the words in sentences.
- Use a timer to see how quickly each sight word is recognized. Begin with a small number of cards. Add more cards once increased speed and confidence is achieved.
- Put the sight words in alphabetical order.
- Come up with another word that begins with the same sound as each sight word.

am	big
box	ran
let	got
play	ball

hat	call
jump	sat
red	black
yellow	green

white	blue
brown	color
say	ask
friend	way

may	today
girl	look
find	dog
run	sit

yes	four
five	six
seven	eight
nine	ten

money	buy
under	upon
next	near
high	tree

found	until
into	same
hard	part
round	fat

funny	might
saw	only
such	never
live	house

home	mother
sister	brother
each	own
name	year

also	fall
sleep	morning
night	bed
o'clock	early

school	open
close	leave
off	door
don't	read

book	over
another	because
car	far
ride	around

back	away
town	took
every	anything
think	people

could	too
men	woman
along	stop
both	walk

clean	wash
water	carry
hot	warm
clothes	coat

cold	kind
dress	better
please	tell
once	use

made	fly
fast	goes
try	though
why	food

ate	full
most	more
always	write
letter	dear

love	yesterday
soon	fine
cut	grow
longer	keep

want	than
should	these
thing	while
which	set

first	second
third	last
order	stand
where	does

those	now
seem	shall
eyes	ear
hear	face

hand	head
fire	sure
start	hold
show	hope

right	left
myself	help
small	pair
come	gave

pretty	present
bring	sing
happy	wish
thank	didn't

end	best

Fry Instant Sight Word List

First One Hundred Words

a	can	her	many	see	us
about	come	here	me	she	very
after	day	him	much	so	was
again	did	his	my	some	we
all	do	how	new	take	were
an	down	I	no	that	what
and	eat	if	not	the	when
any	for	in	of	their	which
are	from	is	old	them	who
as	get	it	on	then	will
at	give	just	one	there	with
be	go	know	or	they	work
been	good	like	other	this	would
before	had	little	our	three	you
boy	has	long	out	to	your
but	have	make	put	two	
by	he	man	said	up	

Fry Instant Sight Word List

Second One Hundred Words

also	color	home	must	red	think
am	could	house	name	right	too
another	dear	into	near	run	tree
away	each	kind	never	saw	under
back	ear	last	next	say	until
ball	end	leave	night	school	upon
because	far	left	only	seem	use
best	find	let	open	shall	want
better	first	live	over	should	way
big	five	look	own	soon	where
black	found	made	people	stand	while
book	four	may	play	such	white
both	friend	men	please	sure	wish
box	girl	more	present	tell	why
bring	got	morning	pretty	than	year
call	hand	most	ran	these	
came	high	mother	read	thing	

Fry Instant Sight Word List

Third One Hundred Words

along	didn't	food	keep	sat	though
always	does	full	letter	second	today
anything	dog	funny	longer	set	took
around	don't	gave	love	seven	town
ask	door	goes	might	show	try
ate	dress	green	money	sing	turn
bed	early	grow	myself	sister	walk
brown	eight	hat	now	sit	warm
buy	every	happy	o'clock	six	wash
car	eyes	hard	off	sleep	water
carry	face	head	once	small	woman
clean	fall	hear	order	start	write
close	fast	help	pair	stop	yellow
clothes	fat	hold	part	ten	yes
coat	fine	hope	ride	thank	yesterday
cold	fire	hot	round	third	
cut	fly	jump	same	those	

Answer Key

Directions: Write the words below. Say them as you write them.

am am
big big
box box

Directions: Write the missing word in each sentence.

1. I am good at playing with my dog.
2. My dog is big.
3. He is in a box.

Now, write a sentence with these words in it: big box

Answers will vary.

5

Directions: Write the words below. Say them as you write them.

ran ran
let let
got got

Directions: Write the missing word in each sentence.

1. I got a dog.
2. He ran in the yard.
3. I let him lick me.

Now, write a sentence with these words in it: dog got

Answers will vary.

6

Directions: Find and circle the words from the box. Words can go → or ↓.

b	o	x	s	l	
i	r	u	n	t	
g	a	m	g	o	
t	n	r	o	n	
e	l	e	t	o	

am
big
box
ran
let
got

Directions: Draw a line to connect the words that rhyme.

ran — can
box — fox
got — hot

7

Directions: Write the words below. Say them as you write them.

play play
ball ball
hat hat

Directions: Circle the word that rhymes with the underlined word in each sentence.

1. The boy can play. (day) dog pup
2. He has a ball. bat (tall) bug
3. He has a hat. hot (bat) ball

8

Directions: Write the words below. Say them as you write them.

call call
jump jump
sat sat

Directions: Write the missing word in each sentence.

1. The frog can jump.
2. He sat by the pond.
3. I will not call to him.
4. Call rhymes with **ball**.

9

Directions: Circle each set of footballs that have rhyming words on them.

play day
ball bat
jump bump
sat mat
hat have
call tall
jump jog
ball all
play pop
hat bat
cat call
is sat

10

Directions: Write the words below. Say them as you write them.

red red
black black
yellow yellow
green green

Directions: Write the missing word in each sentence.

1. A bear is black.
2. An apple is red/yellow/green

11

Directions: Write the words below. Say them as you write them.

white white
blue blue
brown brown
color color

Directions: Write the missing word in each sentence.

white	blue	brown	color

1. I can color the bear brown.
2. The snowman is white.

12

Answer Key

Directions:
1. Color bear number 1 blue.
2. Color bear number 2 green.
3. Color bear number 3 brown.
4. Color bear number 4 yellow.
5. Color bear number 5 white.
6. Color bear number 6 black.
7. Color bear number 7 red.

13

Directions: Write the words below. Say them as you write them.

say say
ask ask
friend friend

Directions: The words **say, ask,** and **friend** are hiding in the lines below. Find and circle them. Now, color the boxes.

a s a y a s a y s a a s a y s y
s a k s a s k a s s a s k a s k
r e i n d f r i e n d f r e n d

14

Directions: Write the words below. Say them as you write them.

way way
may may
today today

Directions: Write the missing word in each sentence. Now, circle the words in each sentence that rhyme.

1. This is the way I want to play.
2. May say this?
3. Today is Monday.

Directions: Write 3 more words that rhyme with **way** and **may**.

Answers will vary.

15

Directions: The letters in the words are mixed up. Unscramble them to write each word correctly. Use the words from the box to help you.

today way ask say friend

1. ksa ask
2. yas say
3. drfeni friend
4. doayt today
5. wya way

Directions: Unscramble the words in this sentence. Now, write the sentence.
I play with my drfeni.

I play with my friend.

16

Directions: Write the words below. Say them as you write them.

girl girl
look look
find find

Directions:
1. Circle the box that says **look**.
2. Color the box that says **find**.
3. Put an **X** on the box that says **girl**.

girl like find
fun look boy

Directions: Circle the two words in each row that are the same.

love	look	like	look
find	four	five	find
girl	girl	got	goat

17

Directions: Write the words below. Say them as you write them.

dog dog
run run
sit sit
yes yes

Directions: Find and circle the dog bones with the words from the box on them.

dog run sit yes

yes ran dog yet set run day sit

How many did you circle? 4

18

Directions: Use the words from the box to write the missing word in each sentence.

girl look find dog run sit yes

1. A girl had a dog.
2. He liked to run fast.
3. One day she lost her dog.
4. She could not find him.
5. She had to look for him. Did she find him?
6. Yes, she did.
7. Now she wants him to sit.

19

Directions: Write the words below. Say them as you write them.

four four
five five
six six
seven seven
eight eight

Directions: Draw a line to the number that matches the word.

six 4
four 8
five 6
seven 5
eight 7

20

Answer Key

Directions: Write the words below. Say them as you write them.

nine	nine
ten	ten
money	money
buy	buy

Directions: Write the missing word in each sentence. Then, write the answers.

1. Can she buy a pencil?
2. How much money does she have?

21

Directions: Draw a line from each box to the word that tells how many coins there are.

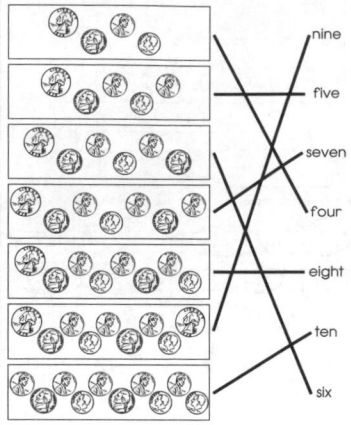

22

Directions: Write the words below. Say them as you write them.

under	under
upon	upon
next	next
near	near

Directions: Write the missing word in each sentence.

1. The rock is under/near a tree.
2. The frog sits upon a lily pad.
3. The mouse is next to the elephant.

23

Directions: Write the words below. Say them as you write them.

high	high
tree	tree
found	found

Directions: Unscramble the letters to make the words from the box. Now, write the correct word next to each apple.

ghhi — high

etre — tree

dnofu — found

24

Directions: Write the words below. Say them as you write them.

until	until
into	into
same	same

Directions: Color the apples that have the same words on them.

under until

into into

same some

same same

into onto

until until

26

Directions: Write the words below. Say them as you write them.

hard	hard
part	part
round	round

Directions: Draw a line to connect the bouncing balls to get to the basket. Use the words from the box.

round hard part

part rode round past hand hard part hard round

27

Directions: Write the missing word in each sentence.

until into same hard round

1. An apple is round/hard
2. It is hard/round
3. You can bite into it.
4. Eat it all until it is gone.
5. The two parts are the same.

Directions: Color the spaces that have words that rhyme with the word in the middle.

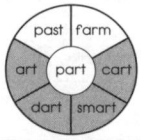

28

Directions: Write the words below. Say them as you write them.

fat	fat
funny	funny
might	might

Directions: Draw a line to connect the words that rhyme.

fat — night

funny — bunny

might — cat

Now, draw a fat, funny mouse.

Pictures will vary.

29

Answer Key

Directions: Write the words below. Say them as you write them.

saw saw
only only
such such
never never

Directions: The words **saw**, **only**, **such**, and **never** are hiding in the boxes below. Find them and color the boxes that have these words in them.

one	only	on	only
saw	was	sun	saw
much	such	such	more
never	ever	never	even

30

Directions: Find and circle the words from the box. Words can go → or ↓.

fat
funny
might
saw
only
such
never

f	a	t	n	m	n
u	t	i	g	l	e
n	h	v	e	g	v
n	s	u	c	h	e
y	a	n	g	t	r
l	w	o	n	l	y

Directions: Color the spaces that have words that rhyme with the word in the middle of the circle.

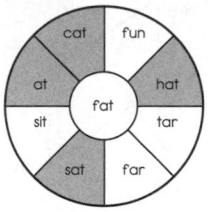

31

Directions: Write the words below. Say them as you write them.

live live
house house
home home

Directions: The letters on the houses are mixed up. Unscramble them to write each word. Use the words from the box to help you.

live house home

house home live

32

Directions: Write the words below. Say them as you write them.

mother mother
sister sister
brother brother

Directions: Select the word from the box that answers these riddles.

mother sister brother

I am a girl. sister

I am a boy. brother

I am a woman. mother

Pictures will vary.

Now, draw a picture of yourself.

33

Directions: Find and circle the words from the box. Words can go → or ↓.

live
house
home
mother
sister

m	s	m	h	t	l
o	i	u	o	e	r
t	s	s	u	h	l
h	t	o	s	t	i
e	e	u	e	o	v
r	r	h	o	m	e

Directions: Draw a picture of where you live.

Pictures will vary.

34

each own name year also fall

Directions: Find the leaves that have the words from the box on them. Color them these colors:

each = red **own** = green **name** = yellow
year = orange **also** = brown

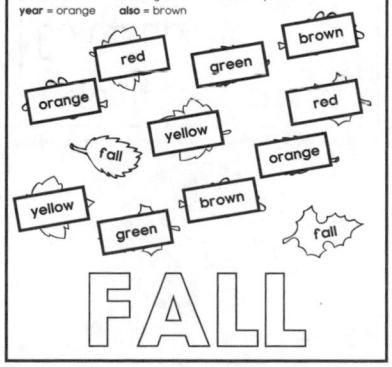

37

Directions: Write the words below. Say them as you write them.

o'clock o'clock
early early
school school

Directions: Read the sentences and follow the directions.

1. Write **one** under the star with the word **o'clock** on it.
2. Write **two** under the star with the word **school** on it.
3. Write **three** under the star with the word **early** on it.

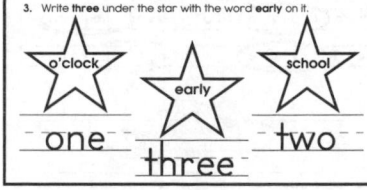

39

Directions: Read the story. Now, find and circle the words that are in the box.

sleep morning night bed
o'clock early school

I have to go to bed at eight o'clock at night. I do not like to go to sleep too early. In the morning I have to get up. When I get up, my dog is there. He wants to go on a walk. So I walk with him before I go to school.

What time do you go to bed? Show it on the clock and write the time on the line.

Answers will vary.

40

Answer Key

Directions: Write the words below. Say them as you write them.

off off
door door
don't don't

Directions: Write the missing word in each sentence. Use the words from the box to help you.

off	door	don't

1. I will turn off the light.
2. Don't close the door.
3. The door is open.

42

Directions: Read the story. Now, find and circle the words from the box.

open	close	leave
off	door	don't

One night I had to leave the door open. I do not like the dark, so I said, "Mom, don't close the door." Then I said, Don't turn the light off. Then I went to sleep.

Directions: Draw a line to connect words that are opposites.

on — don't
open — off
do — close

43

Directions: Write the words below. Say them as you write them.

read
book
over

Directions: Several words below are mixed up. Unscramble the letters and write all the words on the lines. Use the words from the box.

book	over	read	and	can	I	a

I nac daer a kobo
I can read a book
voer dna voer.
over and over

44

Directions: Use the words from the box to complete the story.

read	book	over
another	because	

The girl is sitting in a chair. She likes to read her book here. She will even read another book, too. She has lots of books because she likes to read. She will read her books over again.

Directions: Circle the books with the same words on them.

read red
book book
anything another
over over
read read
book look

46

Directions: Write the words below. Say them as you write them.

car car
far far
ride ride
around around

Directions: Color the cars that have words that rhyme with **ride**.

head
rode
wide
dear
hide
said
side
read
tide

47

Directions: Write the words below. Say them as you write them.

back back
away away
town town
took took

Directions: Read each sentence. Circle the word that rhymes with the underlined word.

1. The car went back home.	bag	sack	come
2. Will the bug go away?	rug	fill	stay
3. We went all over town.	too	down	ball
4. It took a long time to get home.	lot	look	song

48

Directions: Find and circle the words from the box. Words can go → or ↓.

car
far ride
around back
away town
took

k	r	a	f	o	o	k
r	d	k	o	o	t	s
f	a	r	d	w	o	r
a	w	o	f	e	w	i
c	a	r	o	u	n	d
y	y	l	r	t	b	e

Directions: The words **town** and **ride** are hiding in the boxes below. Find and circle them.

w	n	t	o	w	n	t	o	n	w	o	t	o	w	n

e	d	r	i	d	e	r	i	d	r	i	d	e	e	d	e

49

Directions: Write the words below. Say them as you write them.

every every
anything anything
think think

Directions: Color the spaces that have the same word as the one in the middle of the circle.

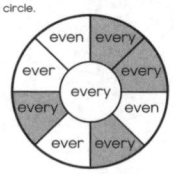

How many spaces did you color? 4

50

Answer Key

Directions: Write the words below. Say them as you write them.

people people
could could
too too

Directions: Unscramble the letters to make the words from the box. Now, write them on the line under each book.

could people too

oto eopple dcluo

too people could

Now, write this sentence.
People could read too.

People could read too.

51

Directions: Read the story. Now, find and circle the words from the box.

every anything think people could too

I love to read every book I can.
I tell my friends that they could too.
They could read as many books as I do.
I think lots of people could read anything
they want. Let's read!

Now, write a sentence telling what you think people would like to read about.

Answers will vary.

52

Directions: Write the words below. Say them as you write them.

men men
woman woman
along along

Directions: Color the spaces that have the same word as the one in the middle of the circle.

mend men
men men
man men mend
men men

How many spaces did you color? 5

53

Directions: Write the words below. Say them as you write them.

stop stop
both both
walk walk

Directions: Look at the picture. Which sentence tells about the picture? Put an **X** by that sentence.

1. ____ Both men are driving a car.
2. ____ Both men will stop eating.
3. X Both men walk by the stop sign.
4. ____ The men both jump.

54

Directions: To get to the street, draw a line to connect the stop signs that contain the words from the box. The first one is done for you.

men woman along stop both walk

talk both woman top
women man stop alone
walk along men ball

25

55

Directions: Write the words below. Say them as you write them.

clean clean
wash wash
water water

Directions: Unscramble the words on the wash tubs. Now, write each word on the line. Use the words from the box to help you.

swha retwa enacl

wash water clean

Now, write this sentence.
Wash with clean water.

Wash with clean water.

56

Directions: Write the words below. Say them as you write them.

carry cary
hot hot
warm warm

Directions: Draw a line from each bucket to its matching word.

carrot carry cart carry
hot hop lot hot
wash what water water

57

Directions: Unscramble the words from the box. Write each word on the line under its bubble. Now, write the words on the wash tubs in alphabetical order.

clean wash water hot warm

clean naelc hwas
hot clean wash
warm rweat toh
wash water hot
water awrm warm

58

Directions: Write the words below. Say them as you write them.

clothes clothes
coat coat
cold cold

Directions: Color the spaces that have words that rhyme with the same word in the middle of the circle.

bold coat cod doll cold told old colt hold

How many spaces did you color? 4

59

Directions: Write the words below. Say them as you write them.

kind kind
dress dress
better better

Directions: The words **kind**, **dress**, and **better** are hidden in the lines below. Find and circle them. Now, color the boxes.

k n d k i n d n k i n d n i k n
r s e d s r d r e s s d r e s s
b e b e t t e r b t b e t t e r

60

Directions: Find and circle the words from the box. Words can go → or ↓.

clothes
coat
cold
kind
dress
better

r	c	k	i	n	d
b	l	r	c	o	r
e	o	h	o	o	e
t	t	a	a	c	s
t	h	m	t	h	s
e	e	p	e	s	r
r	s	c	o	l	d

Directions: Draw a line to connect each word to its picture.

1. kind
2. coat
3. clothes
4. dress
5. cold
6. better

61

Directions: Write the words below. Say them as you write them.

please please
tell tell
once once

Directions: Write the missing word in each sentence. Use the words from the box to help you.

once tell please

1. Will you please close the door?
2. I can tell time.
3. Once, I fell in a lake.

62

Directions: Write the words below. Say them as you write them.

use use
made made

Directions: Write the missing word in each sentence. Use the words from the box to help you.

use made

1. He made a home run hit.
2. I will use the bat to hit the ball.

Directions: Color the spaces that have the same word as the one in the middle of the circle.

you up use use use use see

63

Directions: Read the story. Now, find and circle the words from the box.

once tell use please made

Once, I wanted to hear a story. I said, "Dad, please tell me one."

Dad said, "Once upon a time, there was a baby duck. It liked to play in the water. Once, a day it made a mess. The mother duck said, "That is the last time I let you use the pond to swim in!"

Directions: Unscramble the words on the eggs.

letl econ emda
tell once made
easlpe seu
please use

64

Directions: Write the words below. Say them as you write them.

fly fly
fast fast
goes goes

Directions: Color the spaces that have the same word as the one in the middle of the circle.

good gone goes goes goes gone good goes goes

Now, write this sentence.
A plane can fly fast.

A plane can fly fast.

65

Directions: Write the words below. Say them as you write them.

try try
though though
why why

Directions: Write the missing word in each sentence. Use the words from the box to help you.

try though why

1. I try to tie my shoes.
2. It is hard to do it though.
3. I don't know why it is hard to do.

66

Answer Key

Directions: Find and circle the words from the box. Words can go → or ↓.

fly
fast
goes
try
though
why

s	t	h	o	r	t	w
g	o	e	s	o	e	h
r	y	w	h	t	r	y
a	t	h	o	u	g	h
f	a	s	t	f	a	w
a	o	f	s	l	t	y
w	h	t	r	y	w	h

Directions: Draw a line to connect the planes that have words that rhyme.

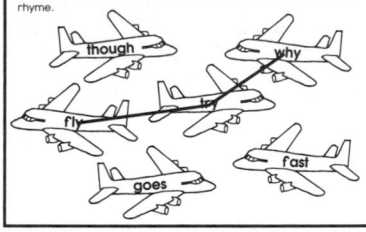

67

Directions: Write the words below. Say them as you write them.

food food
ate ate
full full

Directions: Write the missing word in each sentence.

food ate full

1. I like to eat food.
2. If I eat too much, I get full.
3. Last night, I ate too much.

68

Directions: Write the words below. Say them as you write them.

most most
more more
always always

Directions: Write the missing letters from the words below. Use the words from the box to help you.

most more always

1. mo s t
2. a l way s
3. mo r e

Now, write a sentence using one of the words from the box.

Answers will vary.

69

Directions: Find and circle the words from the box. Words can go → or ↓.

food
ate
full
most
more
always

a	m	o	r	e	d
l	y	f	e	f	a
w	a	t	e	o	m
a	w	t	m	o	o
y	l	l	u	d	s
s	f	u	l	l	t

Directions: Read the story. Now, find and circle the words from the box.

This food is good. I always eat too much. My dad eats the most. One night he ate it all! Now he is always full. He can not eat any more.

70

Directions: Write the words below. Say them as you write them.

write write
letter letter
dear dear
love love

Directions: Answer the questions below using the words from the box.

letter dear

1. What do you send in the mail? letter
2. What word do you use to begin a letter? dear

71

Directions: Color the spaces that have the same word as the one in the middle of the circle.

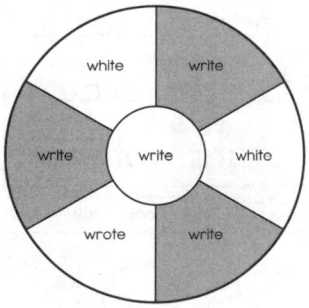

How many did you find? 3

72

Directions: Write the words below. Say them as you write them.

yesterday yesterday
soon soon
fine fine

Directions: Circle the word that is the opposite of the underlined word.

1. I went home yesterday. house **today** no
2. The bus will be here soon. **later** sun hot
3. We are fine. sing song **sick**

Now, write this sentence.
I was fine yesterday.

I was fine yesterday.

73

Directions: Find and circle the words from the box that are in the letter.

write letter dear love yesterday soon fine

Dear Grandmother,
I want to write you a letter today because I miss you. I hope you are fine. Yesterday we went to the zoo. See you soon.
Love, Sam

Now, write a note to someone. Use the words **dear**, **love**, **soon**, and **fine**.

Answers will vary.

74

Directions: Write the words below. Say them as you write them.

cut cut
grow grow
longer longer
keep keep

Directions: Find and circle the words from the box.

cut grow longer keep

gone grow kite
kite cat longer
cat keep
cut gone

75

Directions: Write the words below. Say them as you write them.

want want
than than
should should

Directions: Color the spaces that have the same word as the one in the middle of the circle.

could went
want now
went want could
now want

Now, write a sentence using the word **than** or **should**.

Answers will vary.

76

Directions: Read the story. Find and circle the words from the box.

longer keep want grow
should cut want

I want to cut the grass. I should cut it today because it is going to rain. It is hard to keep it looking good. I want it to grow but the bugs keep eating it. Maybe it will grow longer next year.

Directions: Write the letters that are missing in the words below. Use the words from the box to help you.

c u t g r ow t h a n
k ee p sh o u l d lo n g e r
w a nt

77

Directions: Write the words below. Say them as you write them.

these these
thing thing
while while

Directions: The words **these** and **thing** are hidden in the lines below. Find and circle them.

t h e s t h e s e t h e s t h e
t h i n t h n g t h i n g t h n

How many did you circle of each?

these 1 **thing** 1

78

Directions: Write the words below. Say them as you write them.

which which
set set

Directions: Color the spaces that have the same word as the one in the middle of the circle.

set sit
sat set
set set sat
set sit

How many spaces did you color? 4

79

Directions: Put the correct words on the footprints to complete the sentences below.

thing set
these while which
3 4 5 2

This thing is big. Which animal is here? These are big feet! I will hide while it goes by. I do not want it to knock over my set of blocks.

80

Directions: Write the words below. Say them as you write them.

first first
second second
third third

Directions: Write the word from the box that tells which football it is.

first second third

first second third

Directions: Answer the question below.

What grade are y

Answers will vary.

81

Directions: Write the words below. Say them as you write them.

last last
order order
stand stand

Directions: Answer the questions using the words from the box.

order last stand

1. Circle the dog that is next to last.
2. Color the dog that is on the stand.
3. The dogs are in order. Draw an arrow to show the tallest and the shortest dogs.

82

Answer Key

Directions: Read the sentences to answer the questions about the picture.

Ann Bob Jill Tom Jane

1. Who is in the last row? Ann
2. Who is in the second row? Tom
3. Who is in the third row? Jill
4. Who is in the first row? Jane
5. Draw where you will st

Answers will vary.

83

Directions: Write the words below. Say them as you write them.

where where
does does
those those

Directions: Write the word from the box that is missing in each sentence below.

where does those

1. Does he have his shoes?
2. Are those his socks?
3. Where is his coat?

84

Directions: Write the words below. Say them as you write them.

now now
seem seem
shall shall

Directions: The words **now**, **seem**, and **shall** are hiding in the lines below. Find and circle them. Now, color the boxes.

n w o n o w o w n o w n o n o w
e m e e m s e e m e e s e e m e
s h l l s h a l l s h a l s h a

Directions: What time is it now?

nine o'clock / 9:00

85

Directions: Write the words below. Say them as you write them.

eyes eyes
ear ear
hear hear

Directions: Write the word that is missing in each sentence below.

eyes ear hear

1. I see with my eyes.
2. My ear can help me hear.

Now, draw a picture of your face. Show where your eyes and ears are. Put a label on them.

Pictureswill vary.

87

Directions: Write the words below. Say them as you write them.

face face
hand hand
head head

Directions: Fill in the letters that are missing in the words below.

1. h a n d
2. f a c e
3. h e a d

Now, draw a picture of yourself. Show where your face, hands, and head are. Put labels on your drawing.

Pictures will vary.

88

Directions: Use the words from the box to fill in the labels on the drawing.

eyes ear face hand head

eyes head
ear face hand

Now, write this sentence.
I can hear a train.

I can hear a train.

89

Directions: Write the words below. Say them as you write them.

fire fire
sure sure
start start

Directions: Color the spaces that have the same word as the one in the middle of the circle.

sure: some, sore, sire, sure, some, sore

90

Directions: Write the words below. Say them as you write them.

hold hold
show show
hope hope

Directions: Circle the three words in each row that are the same.

hope	hold	hold	home	hold
shop	ship	show	show	show
home	hope	hope	ham	hope
start	stop	start	store	start

91

Answer Key

Directions: Read the story. Find and circle the words from the box.

start	sure	hold	show	hope	fire

It is cold and time to start a fire. My dad will show us how to start the fire. I hope it gets warm soon. I will hold my hands close to the fire to warm up. My dad says, "Be sure not to get too close."

Now, write this sentence.
I hope he will show us how to hold that.

I hope he will show us how to hold that.

92

Directions: Write the words below. Say them as you write them.

right right
left left
myself myself

Directions: Read the sentences. Now, follow the directions.

1. Circle the dog on the right.
2. Color the dog on the left.
3. Draw an arrow to the cat on the left.
4. Color the cat on the right.

Now, complete this sentence.

I like myself because Answers will vary.

93

Directions: Write the words below. Say them as you write them.

help help
small small
pair pair

Directions: Draw a line to match the pants that have the same words on them.

help	small	pair

Now, write this sentence.
It is a pair of pants.

It is a pair of pants.

94

Directions: Find and circle the words from the box. Words can go → or ↓.

right
left
myself
help
small
pair

m	y	s	e	l	f	f
t	t	l	p	f	r	t
s	m	a	l	l	r	f
g	f	p	e	e	i	e
h	e	l	p	f	g	l
l	s	m	a	t	h	g
p	a	l	r	m	t	h

Directions: Draw a line to connect words that are opposites.

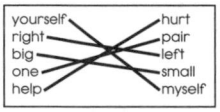

Now, draw a picture of one of the opposite pairs.

Pictures will vary.

95

Directions: Write the words below. Say them as you write them.

present present
bring bring
sing sing

Directions: Color the boxes that have **present**, **bring**, and **sing** in them. Use a different color for each word.

song	present	bang	sing
pretty	bring	song	present
sing	present	bright	sang
present	pretty	sing	bring

How many did you find?

present 4 bring 2 sing 3

97

Directions: Find and circle the words from the box. Words can go → or ↓.

came
gave
pretty
present
bring
sing

g	a	v	e	r	l	y
o	g	a	e	v	n	p
n	v	s	i	n	g	r
c	a	m	e	o	n	e
a	t	p	r	e	i	t
p	r	e	s	e	n	t
b	r	i	n	g	b	y

Directions: Circle the candles that have the words from the box on them.

How many candles did you circle? 6

98

Directions: Write the words below. Say them as you write them.

happy happy
wish wish
thank thank

Directions: Draw a string to tie the balloons together that have the words from the box on them.

happy	wish	thank

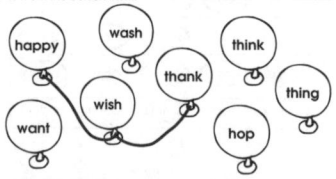

99

Directions: Write the words below. Say them as you write them.

didn't didn't
end end
best best

Directions: Color the boxes that have the words **didn't**, **end**, and **best** in them. Use a different color for each word.

don't	end	send	best
send	best	bet	end
end	bend	rest	didn't
best	didn't	did	send

How many did you find?

didn't 2 end 3 best 3

100

Directions: Read the story. Now, find and circle the words that are in the box.

came	gave	pretty	present	bring	sing
happy	wish	thank	didn't	end	best

It was my birthday. Lots of people came to bring me a present. They also came to sing happy birthday. My mother gave me a pretty dress. My brother gave me a big book. I have to thank them all. I wish the day didn't have to end. It was the best birthday ever!

Now, draw a picture of your favorite birthday present.

Pictures will vary.

101

Answer Key

Page 102

1. I got a dog.
2. He sleeps in a box.
3. My dog is big.
4. He ran in the yard.
5. I let him lick me.

Page 103

1. The girl had a dog.
2. The dog liked to run away fast.
3. The girl had to find the dog.
4. She had to look for him.
5. Did she find him? Yes, she did!
6. Now the girl wants the dog to sit.

Page 104

1. It is dark at night.
2. I get in my bed.
3. I have to go to sleep now.
4. In the morning I get up.
5. I have to get up early.
6. And I have to go to school.

Page 105

1. I see a door.
2. It is open.
3. Don't close the door.
4. Leave the light on.
5. Please don't turn off the light.
6. I don't like the dark.

Page 106

1. We went for a ride.
2. We drove in the car.
3. The ride took a long time.
4. We went far away.
5. Then we went around the park.
6. At last we came back home.

Page 107

1. I have to wash the dishes.
2. I will carry them to the sink.
3. I need to get some water.
4. The water is not too warm.
5. Now the dishes are clean.
6. Now I am done!

Page 108

1. It is cold outside.
2. I better not go outside yet.
3. My dress is not very warm.
4. First, I need to put on some warm clothes.
5. My mom gives me a warm coat.
6. She is very kind to me.

Page 109

1. The food is good here.
2. I always eat too much.
3. My dad eats the most food.
4. He ate all the food on his plate!
5. Now he is full.
6. He can not eat any more.

Page 110

1. Bob wrote a letter to his sister.
2. He wrote, "Dear Pat, how are you?"
3. "I am fine," Bob wrote.
4. "Yesterday I went to the park."
5. He signed it, "Love, Bob."
6. He will mail it soon.

Page 111

1. I can hear the dog bark.
2. I can hear with my ear.
3. I have two eyes.
4. I can see my face in the mirror.
5. My hat is on my head.
6. A hand has five fingers.

Page 113
May I say this?
He likes to run fast.
She had to look for him.
Can she buy a pencil?

Page 114
A rock is under a tree.
I will leave the car.
Please close the door.
Let's get another pumpkin.

Page 115
That plane can fly fast.
My dad eats the most.
A hand has five fingers.
I will write a letter to you.

Page 116
He hit a home run.
I will write a letter soon.
I can see with my eyes.
It goes right here.